Maestro

At Table

Maestro

ANDRÉ TCHELISTCHEFF AND
THE REBIRTH OF NAPA VALLEY

James O. Gump

UNIVERSITY OF NEBRASKA PRESS
Lincoln

Library of Congress
Cataloging-in-Publication Data
Names: Gump, James O. (James Oliver), author.
Title: Maestro: André Tchelistcheff and the
rebirth of Napa Valley / James O. Gump.
Description: Lincoln: University of Nebraska
Press, [2021] | Series: At table | Includes
bibliographical references and index.
Identifiers: LCCN 2020051847
ISBN 9781496226051 (hardback)
ISBN 9781496227089 (epub)
ISBN 9781496227096 (mobi)
ISBN 9781496227102 (pdf)
Subjects: LCSH: Tchelistcheff, André, 1901–
1994. | Vintners—United States—Biography. |
Wine and wine making—California—
Napa Valley—History—20th century.
Classification: LCC TP547.T37 G86
2021 | DDC 663/.20092 [B]—dc23
LC record available at
https://lccn.loc.gov/2020051847

Set in Adobe Jensen by Mikala R. Kolander.
Designed by N. Putens.

For André's students

Contents

Illustrations

Preface

On December 7, 1991, over two hundred friends, family, and wine industry associates from the United States, France, Italy, Germany, and Australia gathered in San Francisco in the Fairmont Hotel's grand ballroom to celebrate the ninetieth birthday of Napa Valley winemaker André Tchelistcheff. Brother Timothy Diener, the cellar master for the Christian Brothers winery for over a half century, provided the invocation, and Dick Maher, president of the Heublein Fine Wine Group, hosted the event. Maher read aloud the birthday greetings sent to André by Ronald and Nancy Reagan, as well as George H. W. and Barbara Bush. Henri Maire, a notable French vintner from Arbois, honored Tchelistcheff with the prestigious Medal of Joseph Capus, founder of France's Institute of Appellations of Origin. The Italian vintner and journalist Gelasio Lovatelli presented André with a sterling silver box engraved with the names of the great producers of Italy. On behalf of Napa Valley's Beaulieu Vineyard (BV), Maher presented Tchelistcheff with a bottle of a '46 BV Pinot Noir, which André regarded as his greatest Burgundian achievement, and a bottle of '47 Georges de Latour Private Reserve Cabernet Sauvignon. A number of André's former students provided tributes. Firestone Vineyard's winemaker Alison Green alluded to André's penchant for sleeping near the wine vats during the harvest and crush to listen closely for "enological sounds." Rob Davis, the winemaker at Jordan Winery, marveled at André's legendary stamina and mocked his mentor's "deceptively gentle" manner. The acclaimed Napa Valley vintner Joe Heitz remarked that "anyone who spends an hour with André and doesn't learn something is a pretty stupid fool." Louis P. Martini, another Napa legend, lauded Tchelistcheff's enological and viticultural skills, and praised André as a "humanitarian, philosopher, teacher, and friend." Napa winemaker Heidi Peterson Barrett, who witnessed the proceedings, later observed that "you would think that you were in the presence of a demigod."[1]

Over the course of his thirty-five-year career as a winemaker at Beaulieu Vineyard, followed by nearly two decades of freelance consulting, André Tchelistcheff (1901–94) became a winemaking legend nationally and internationally. Wine insiders characterized André as the "winemaker's winemaker," the "dean of California winemaking," and the "Maestro." Tchelistcheff's students, who include some of the most accomplished winemakers of the post-Prohibition period, marveled over their mentor's sense of authority, profound insight, humble presence, and abundant wisdom. During André's lifetime, wine critics writing for the *Los Angeles Times*, *San Francisco Chronicle*, *Oakland Tribune*, *Wine Spectator*, *Decanter*, and *Wines & Vines* featured Tchelistcheff in their publications. Most important, André's many admirers regarded him as an essential force in the revitalization of the Napa Valley wine industry following its near-death experience during Prohibition (1920–33). Yet despite Tchelistcheff's legendary reputation and regardless of the accolades André received over his lifetime, no full-length biography of the man exists. It may be in part because of André's lack of pretension and disdain for material possessions, but it is certainly not because his life story was unremarkable or short of accomplishments. *Maestro: André Tchelistcheff and the Rebirth of Napa Valley* attempts to bridge this gap as well as preserve the memory of one of the most influential winemakers of the modern era.

Maestro examines the life and times of a diminutive Russian émigré who brought his Old World experience to California, adapted it to a New World ecology, and mentored others in the technical skills and philosophical approaches to winemaking that were so fundamental to the transformation of American wine culture after Prohibition. It begins and ends with the famous "Tchelistcheff tour" in 1976, the first group of California wine professionals to formally visit the châteaus and vineyards of France. The book then explores André's Russian childhood within the context of the dramatic changes taking place in the Russian Empire during the early twentieth century. It follows the harrowing events that forced the Tchelistcheffs to flee their homeland during the Bolshevik Revolution and examines André's various ordeals during the Russian Civil War and his exile in Europe that followed. During André's exile, he received broad training in agronomy, biochemistry, and animal husbandry, as well as viticulture, and in the 1930s he studied under some of the France's greatest enologists at Paris's Institute of National Agronomy and the Pasteur Institute. After moving his family to Napa Valley in 1938 to become Beaulieu's new enologist-viticulturist, Tchelistcheff applied his expertise in sanitation, agronomy, and fermentation to a winemaking region virtually ruined by Prohibition and willingly shared his ideas with a fledgling group of visionary vintners in the post–World War II era. André left Beaulieu in 1973, several years after its corporate takeover by Heublein, and spent the next two decades as a full-time freelance consultant in California, Washington, Oregon, and Italy. Throughout his professional lifetime and especially in his final years, André's greatest legacy was in mentoring others in the science and poetry of winemaking—on how to use technique and imagination to produce wines of subtlety, harmony, and complexity. In addition, Tchelistcheff taught his many students, both male and female, about empathy, patience, humility, respect, and responsibility. Napa winemaker Warren Winiarski, one of André's star pupils, pointed out that on the one hand, his mentor could be "imperious" and "abrupt." On the other hand, Tchelistcheff was also "poetic," "visionary," and "romantic." André possessed two geniuses, according to Winiarski: "dry-eyed, rigorous exactitude" and "generous leaps of imagination."[2]

Acknowledgments

First and foremost, I wish to thank Dorothy Tchelistcheff for inspiring and supporting me throughout this project, especially when, early on, I nearly decided to abandon it. She related stories about André's Russian background, European exile, experiences as a winemaker and consultant, and traveling adventures to the Pacific Northwest, Europe, and the Caribbean. In addition, Dorothy shared documents, news clippings, and photographs she kept in her home. With my encouragement, she collaborated with Special Collections Library at the University of California (UC), Davis, in 2019 to archive these materials, which are now available to researchers as the Tchelistcheff (Dorothy and André) Collection. I also want to thank the librarians and archivists who assisted me along the way, especially Lynne Albrecht at the St. Helena Public Library and Jullianne Ballou, David Michalski, Alex Borg, and Sara Gunasekara at the Shields Library of UC-Davis. UC-Berkeley's Regional Oral History Office at the Bancroft Library also played a key role in this project by providing electronic access to its extraordinary collection on prominent California wine professionals. At the University of San Diego, where I taught history for thirty-eight years, I want to thank digital graphic artist Allen Wynar and media production assistant Ryan Murphy for their splendid work in mapmaking and cassette digitization. Special thanks also go to Joanne Dickenson DePuy, who led the first group of California wine professionals to France in May 1976 and shared her experiences of that famous tour. I also want to thank Carole Viney, assistant to the president of Chateau Ste. Michelle, for facilitating important interviews in Washington State; Lynda Eller, director of communications at Ste. Michelle, for sharing the company's "family tree"; Darrell Corti, owner and manager of Corti Brothers market in Sacramento, for offering key insights into André's background and career; Maria Tchelistcheff, André's niece, who provided important genealogical information about her family; Andy Beckstoffer, a prominent Napa Valley grape grower, who shared significant details about his experiences on the '76 Tchelistcheff tour in France; Heidi Barrett, Robin Lail, Sean McMeekin, and Richard Peterson, for their informative email correspondence; and Lee Ann Otto, my wife, traveling companion, and discerning participant during each of my winemaker interviews. Finally, I want to extend my abiding gratitude to André's students for sharing stories about their mentor and for assisting me in understanding his contributions to their own careers and to the success of the wine industry in general: Jill Davis, Rob Davis, Alison Green Doran, Alex Golitzin, Doug Gore, Michael Hoffman, Cheryl Barber Jones, Chris Markell, Anne Moller-Racke, Rick Sayre, and Kay Simon. This book is dedicated to them and to the scores of others André mentored over his extraordinary fifty-six-year career.

Maestro

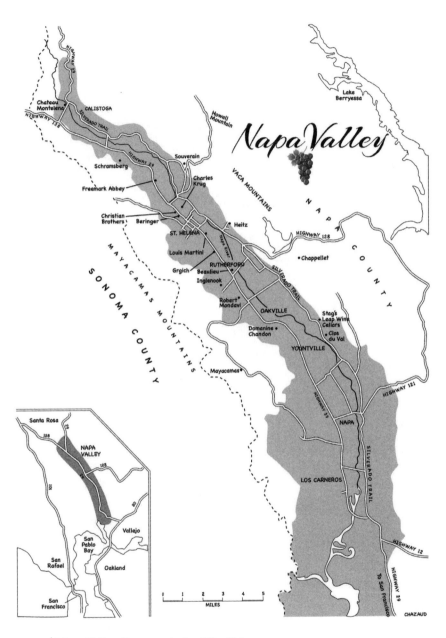

Napa Valley. Cartography by Allen Wynar.

CHAPTER I

The Tchelistcheff Tour, Part 1

Young lady, you have a nucleus of great promise. And
now I will answer all of your questions.

—ANDRÉ TCHELISTCHEFF

When Joanne Dickenson DePuy moved to the city of Napa, California, in 1951, farmers in the valley, which stretched from San Pablo Bay
in the south to Mount St. Helena in the north, harvested nearly as
many prunes as grapes. As she reflected years later, the valley's fame
as a premier wine region, as *the* Napa Valley, awaited its moment.
Regardless, the valley stood out as a special place. First of all, the
region was blessed with a Mediterranean climate, featuring dry, warm
summers and wet, cool winters. Two forested mountain ranges—the
Vaca Mountains in the east and the Mayacamas Mountains in the
west—flanked it, framing a valley floor stretching thirty miles from
north to south and no wider than five miles at any point. In addition
to its conducive climate, the valley's parent soils of volcanic and marine
origin intermingled over millions of years with alluvial fans conveyed
by water from the adjacent mountains. This geological convergence
resulted in some of the most varied soil compositions on Earth. Of
the twelve orders of the world's soil types, Napa Valley contains six
of them, and within them are nearly three dozen different soil series
and over a hundred soil variations. Along with its rich soil diversity,
the valley also receives cooling breezes from the Pacific Ocean and San

Pablo Bay that moderate the summer's midday heat. Furthermore, the valley experiences a significant diurnal temperature fluctuation, with nighttime lows that are often 30–40 degrees Fahrenheit cooler than daytime temperatures. As a result, agriculture typically thrives in Napa Valley, especially in the production of grapes. During good vintages, grapevines grow according to a natural "rhythm of nighttime rest and daytime photosynthesis," resulting in ripe, flavorful grapes capable of producing wines of purity, elegance, and complexity.[1]

After moving to Napa, Joanne spent most of the next two decades as a housewife and mother, with part-time work in a travel agency outside of the home. Her status changed dramatically in the early 1970s, however, when a divorce prompted Joanne to search for a more permanent career. The path she chose blended her interest in international relations, which was her undergraduate major at UC-Berkeley, with her twin passions for tennis and wine. In 1974 Joanne, then engaged to be married to Newell DePuy Jr., founded Tennis Limited and Wine Tours International. Joanne's good friend Molly Chappellet, the wife of the winemaker Donn Chappellet, helped her assemble a clientele for international tennis tours. Some of her early recruits included celebrities such as Clint Eastwood and Nancy Sinatra. Recruiting wealthy tennis aficionados to participate in glamourous international tours was one thing, but the world of wine was another political animal altogether. As a result, Joanne's recruitment efforts for Wine Tours International required an assist from wine industry insiders, so she decided to reach out to the Napa Valley Vintners association. Joanne did not fully understand the politics of the wine industry, which was dominated by men; therefore, she approached her task apprehensively. Joanne believed that as a young businesswoman she had to be careful and "know how to play the game."[2]

At the time, Louis P. Martini served as the president of the Napa Valley Vintners association and was Joanne's principal point of contact. Martini's father, Louis M., came to California from Genoa, Italy, at the age of twelve to join his father, Agostino, who had established a seafood business on San Francisco Bay and started a small winery following the San Francisco earthquake and fire of 1906. Seeking to upgrade his winemaking skills, Agostino's son returned to Italy in 1907 to study enology, an experience that convinced him to pursue a career of making wine and selling it. Louis M. moved back to California in 1911, married Assunta Boragni in 1917, and formed the Louis M. Martini Grape Products Company in the San Joaquin Valley five years later. During Prohibition, his company produced medicinal and sacramental wines, concentrates, and brandy, once selling 100,000 gallons of wine in one day. Just prior to Prohibition's repeal, Martini moved his family to the Napa Valley, establishing the Louis M. Martini Winery on the St. Helena Highway in 1933. As his modest winery known for its quality table wines evolved into a multimillion-dollar business over the years, Martini became one of the original founders of the Napa Valley Vintners, which was established in 1944.[3]

His son Louis P., a gentle giant at six feet four, grew up in the wine business and studied enology during his senior year at UC-Berkeley, where he graduated in 1941. After serving as an ordnance officer with the U.S. Army Air Forces during World War II, Martini returned to the family winery to serve as its vice president and production manager. In 1954 the younger Martini took over as the head winemaker, became a highly accomplished one, and succeeded as president and general manager of the Louis M. Martini Winery in 1968. Uneasy about reaching out to Louis P. Martini directly, Joanne instead contacted Martini's wife, Liz. Liz Martini arranged a meeting for Joanne and Louis in September 1974. Joanne's initial encounter with Louis P. put all of her initial apprehensions to rest. Emboldened by Martini's gracious and self-effacing demeanor, Joanne launched enthusiastically into her plan for Wine Tours International, which she envisioned as a "wine bridge" between Napa Valley and other wine regions of the world. Martini was impressed and arranged for Joanne to present her concept to a meeting of the Napa Valley Vintners the following month. Martini also advised her to approach his good friend and highly respected winemaker André Tchelistcheff to lead the tours, knowing that André would bring instant credibility to her project.[4]

Once again, Joanne experienced a certain level of anxiety in reaching out to another iconic winemaker, but she gathered the courage to set up an appointment to meet André. When Joanne arrived at the Tchelistcheff's modest one-story home on Stonecrest Drive in Napa, André's wife Dorothy greeted her at the door and invited Joanne to take a seat in the living room. Joanne awaited nervously. André was in the kitchen mentoring a young winemaker, a familiar role for Tchelistcheff. André finally appeared, pulled up a stool, and in his thick Franco-Russian accent asked, "All right, young lady, what do you have to tell me?" Joanne told André about her businesses, of her goal of establishing a wine bridge, and of how little she knew about or understood the wine industry. André listened patiently but said nothing for nearly forty-five minutes. Flustered, Joanne eventually stopped talking and waited for what seemed an eternity for some kind of response. André finally spoke: "Young lady, you have a nucleus of great promise. And now I will answer all of your questions." André spoke nonstop for thirty minutes before telling Joanne he was too busy to lead a tour at that time, despite that she had not yet even raised the question. André recommended that she contact J. Leland (Lee) Stewart, one of the valley's most respected vintners, who had recently retired from his Souverain winery.[5]

Stewart happily agreed to join Joanne's venture, and over the next year, he led successful wine tours to Argentina and France. Despite her company's efficacious launch, Joanne persisted in trying to convince André Tchelistcheff to lead one of her tours. One summer day in 1975, Joanne encountered André and Dorothy at Vallerga's Market in Napa and half-teasingly asked André when he would lead one of her industry tours to France. "I am ready," André pronounced, "although Dorothy [which he pronounced DOE-lee] will kill me." When they arrived at the checkout stand, Joanne confirmed again that André was on board for the France trip, prompting Dorothy to exclaim, "André, are you out of your mind?" Outside the store, André turned to Dorothy and said, "What did you let me do that for?" With André committed, the Tchelistcheff tour that Joanne dreamed about was now going to be a reality. Working with André, she scheduled a three-week tour to France between May 6 and May 28, 1976. She limited the trip to individuals in the wine industry and knew that André's name would attract an all-star entourage.[6]

In September 1975, as Joanne was preparing for a trip to France to finalize plans for the Tchelistcheff tour, she received a phone call from Patricia Gastaud-Gallagher. An American, Gastaud-Gallagher worked as an assistant with Englishman Steven Spurrier, who owned a wine shop in Paris and directed an adjacent wine school, Académie du Vin. Hired by Spurrier in 1972, Patricia had organized annual tastings of American wines each Fourth of July at the académie to introduce the French to America's best. Unfortunately, America's "best," which Patricia collected from friends in the American Embassy, often left much to be desired. With America's bicentennial approaching in 1976, Gastaud-Gallagher wanted to feature wines of quality that could actually impress even France's most esteemed wine experts. Unconfirmed reports at the time suggested that Napa Valley wineries might be producing some of America's top wines, but Gastaud-Gallagher and Spurrier needed help finding them. Through a friend, Patricia learned about Joanne's Wine Tours International, so she phoned the Napa-based tour director for advice. Joanne shared her enthusiasm for some excellent wines she had recently tasted at Stag's Leap Wine Cellars and Chateau Montelena Winery. Hence, when Patricia flew to San Diego, California, in the fall of 1975 to visit her sister, she traveled north for a brief wine-tasting tour of Napa Valley. For Patricia, two wineries stood out: Stag's Leap Wine Cellars and Chateau Montelena Winery. Upon her return to France, Patricia recalls, "I did not bring samples but I gave Steven my impressions." Spurrier started planning his own trip to Napa Valley for the following spring.[7]

Spurrier and his wife, Bella, visited California in April 1976, making forays into Monterey, Santa Clara, and Sonoma Counties and securing

DePuy as their tour guide when they visited Napa Valley. Outside of Napa Valley, Spurrier came away most impressed with the wines at Chalone Vineyard, Ridge Vineyard, and David Bruce Winery. Upon their arrival in Napa, Joanne drove the Spurriers up into the valley and its surrounding hillsides, visiting Clos du Val, Stag's Leap Wine Cellars, Heitz Wine Cellars, Freemark Abbey, Chateau Montelena, Spring Mountain, and Mayacamas Vineyards. Steven declined stopping at the more noteworthy wineries such as Robert Mondavi Winery, Inglenook, and Beaulieu Vineyard, preferring instead the smaller, off-the-radar establishments. Spurrier told Joanne that he and Patricia Gastaud-Gallagher were hosting a special tasting in Paris that May to honor America's bicentennial and that they wanted to feature some of these excellent American wines. In a blind tasting, he wanted to match six California Cabernet Sauvignons with four Bordeaux red wines and six California Chardonnays beside four Burgundy whites. Spurrier did not envision the tasting as a contest, nor did he think that California wines could surpass France's best Bordeaux and Burgundies. The tasters he recruited for the event ranked among France's leading wine experts and included Aubert de Villaine, the co-owner of the famous winery Domaine de la Romanée-Conti; Odette Kahn, the editor of the *Revue du vin de France*; and Pierre Bréjoux, the inspector general of France's Appellation d'Origine Côntrolée Board.[8]

Joanne liked Spurrier, whom she regarded as a charming, well-dressed Englishman with "an incredible palate." Spurrier also impressed her by paying full price for the bottles he purchased rather than insisting on a merchant discount, a courtesy Joanne had rarely seen on her wine tours. Joanne later found distressing popular depictions of Steven in films such as *Bottle Shock* (2008), which characterizes him as a self-parodying wine snob. When Clos du Val renamed its winery driveway "Steven Spurrier Lane" in 2018, Joanne emailed her congratulations to Spurrier. He replied, "Fame at last!"[9]

Prior to the Tchelistcheff tour, Joanne embarked on the aforementioned planning trip to Paris to meet with Pierre Bréjoux. On this trip she would also meet with Jean Claude Murat, the director of the organization of French travel agents, who played a crucial role in the tour's logistics. Joanne needed Bréjoux's blessing for the Tchelistcheff tour to proceed, so she wanted to impress. Her friends Claude and Ardath Rouas, slated to lead a tennis and-wine trek to France and Britain in 1978, joined her on the Paris trip. Since Joanne did not speak French, she relied on Ardath, an elegant fashion model with bilingual fluency. Bréjoux welcomed the Californians and expressed enthusiasm for the potential benefits of a genuine cultural exchange. Bréjoux's quarrelsome aide, however, who assumed that neither woman spoke French, lashed out at "these Americans who were out to steal France's wine secrets." Joanne's suggestion that the tour include picnic lunches especially irritated Bréjoux's aide, who regarded picnics as retrograde and undignified. Ignoring his colleague's arrogant rants, Bréjoux happily lent his support for Joanne's proposed winery tour.[10]

Six days before the Tchelistcheff tour group departed for France, Joanne received a frantic phone call from Steven Spurrier. "Help!" he said. "I can't take all the wine I bought in California with me to Paris. We are only allowed two bottles each. Can you take the rest with your group?" In case of breakage, Spurrier wanted two bottles of each wine he purchased in California, so he needed at least twenty-four bottles. Joanne agreed to transport the wine but quickly regretted her friendly gesture since she had no idea how to navigate the logistics of getting the wines into France. She decided to reach out to Larry Cahn, the president of the Wine Institute in San Francisco. Cahn had earlier helped Joanne compile a list of potential wine tour clients, so she thought he might also be able to assist her in sorting through wine customs regulations and air travel import codes. Cahn advised Joanne to assign two bottles each to the members of her tour group as a potential way of clearing French customs. Next Joanne contacted Earl Harkin, a Trans World Airlines (TWA) representative with whom she had been working for over a year. Fortunately for Joanne, TWA was also keen on the idea of developing a wine bridge between the world's major wine-producing regions, exactly the purpose Joanne envisioned for Wine Tours International. Harkin promised to assist Joanne in transporting three boxes of wine from San Francisco to Paris via Boston. Now convinced that she could accommodate Steven's request, Joanne phoned André and told him about Spurrier's plan for a comparative tasting of California wines. André wanted to know what wines were being shipped, so Joanne read him the list. "I've never heard of this Steven Spurrier," André replied, "but he has a great palate."[11]

On the morning of May 7, 1976, thirty-five members of the Tchelistcheff tour group, accompanied by Joanne, deplaned at the Charles de Gaulle Airport northeast of Paris with three cases of wine in tow. Spurrier, dressed in a white summer suit and anxious to retrieve his precious cargo, met them at the baggage claim. Joanne spotted the wine cases on the roundabout, "and then I smelled it . . . wine . . . strong wine . . . a magnificent bouquet making its debut in Paris." DePuy feared the worst. As far as she knew, every carefully wrapped bottle of California wine had shattered en route to France. Spurrier seemed unalarmed and quickly discovered that only one bottle—a Freemark Abbey Cabernet Sauvignon—had broken in transit. He then escorted the group through French customs and accompanied it to the Chemin des Vignes, a Parisian wine storage cellar he co-owned. After a wine tasting and light lunch, Spurrier bid adieu to Joanne's tour group, which departed for the hotel. The next day, the study trip billed as "André Tchelistcheff's Tour of France" embarked on its three-week journey to wineries in Champagne, Burgundy, Beaujolais, and Bordeaux.[12]

Shortly after André agreed to lead the 1976 Tchelistcheff tour, Joanne raced into her house and phoned Louis P. Martini with the exciting news. Martini responded, "Sign us up." Joanne's excitement stands to reason. Over his career, André had earned some of winemaking's most prestigious awards. In July 1954, the French government had conferred upon André its highest award in agriculture, the Chevalier du Mérite Agricole, for his contribution in helping bring France's qualitative philosophy of winemaking to America and promoted him to officier du mérite agricole in 1979. In 1970 the American Society of Enologists (known as the American Society for Enology and Viticulture beginning in 1984) had presented Tchelistcheff, one of its charter members, the Merit Award and given him the title "Winemaker's Winemaker."[13] The *Wine Spectator* would bestow upon André its Distinguished Service Award in 1986 and follow it with its Reader's Choice Award in 2000. Finally, Napa's Culinary Institute of America at Copia would honor Tchelistcheff with a Lifetime Achievement Award in 2004 and induct him into its Vintners Hall of Fame in 2007, recognizing him as "the father of modern California winemaking." A bronze statue of André sculpted by William Behrends greets every visitor entering Beaulieu Vineyard's courtyard next to its reserve tasting room. A fiberglass replica also graces the main hallway at the Copia branch campus of the Culinary Institute of America located next to the city of Napa's Oxbow Public Market.

A diminutive Russian émigré, André, despite his slight stature at barely five feet tall, was a giant in the world of wine. Tchelistcheff came to Napa Valley via France in 1938 in the aftermath of Prohibition. The Volstead Act of 1919, which enforced the Eighteenth Amendment to the U.S. Constitution, imposed severe restrictions on the manufacture, transportation, and sale of intoxicating liquors from 1920 until its repeal in 1933. According to wine editor Jon Bonné, this legislation represented "a death sentence for California's wine industry." Its real damage, in Bonné's view, was not economic but cultural: "Decades' worth of winemaking knowledge was lost."[14] Tchelistcheff contributed significantly in restoring that culture, bringing technical skills and a philosophical approach to winemaking that played a major role in filling this cultural void. Warren Winiarski, who founded Stag's Leap Wine Cellars in Napa Valley, reasoned that André "was the scientist and the poet combined. He combined in himself the precision of someone who did very exacting work as well as the vision of someone whose mind could freely flow in directions that no one had anticipated."[15]

Winemaker Richard (Dick) Peterson, who worked side by side with Tchelistcheff at Beaulieu Vineyard from 1968 to 1973, observed that André bridged the gap between grape growing and winemaking, thus personifying the consummate "winegrower."[16] Ruth Teiser, a wine historian, reportedly once said that André bridged European winemaking techniques with those of California.[17] In effect, André Tchelistcheff was the personification of Joanne Depuy's conceptual wine bridge: André brought together the Old World and the New, the science and the poetry, and the exactitude and finesse of winemaking.

Maestro examines Tchelistcheff's pre-California roots as well as his fundamental role in reshaping the Napa Valley wine industry in the post-repeal era. André's unique background—a sickly child, a Russian émigré forced from his homeland during the Bolshevik Revolution, a White Army lieutenant who fought in the Crimea, a physical laborer in a Bulgarian coal mine, a Czechoslovakian-trained agronomist, and a French-schooled viticulturist and enologist—prepared Tchelistcheff for a remarkable thirty-five-year winemaking career in Napa Valley's Beaulieu Vineyard and nearly two "post-retirement" decades of freelance consulting work for over thirty wineries. Among his most significant achievements, Tchelistcheff introduced the cold fermentation process for white and rosé wines, advocated for the use of controlled malolactic fermentation in red wines, adopted European methods of cultivating and pruning vineyards, developed widely used frost protection techniques, and pioneered the use of the laboratory as an indispensable winemaking tool.[18]

More important, Tchelistcheff's early struggles forged his principal character traits, which he applied to the art and science of winemaking as well as to life in general. These characteristics, which he modeled to an entire generation of winemakers, included Tchelistcheff's romantic spirit, intellectual curiosity, love of nature, youthful energy, lack of pretension, and disdain for material possessions. Above all, André's empathy for others stands out as one of his most notable core values and is reflected in his commitment to teach and mentor. In that role,

André helped bridge the gender gap in the winemaking profession, inspiring several generations of women and men to pursue their careers with passion, integrity, and total commitment. Winemaker Jill Davis said that André had a "gentle manner of teaching me all the important things." In particular, André taught her to practice "conscious winemaking" by paying constant attention to what the wine was telling her and attending to issues immediately. "He was a great teacher," winemaker Rob Davis said. "He had so much knowledge and wisdom. To know André was like looking in the back of a book that has all the answers." Another student of André's, winemaker Miljenko (Mike) Grgich, said that Tchelistcheff "had such a tremendous horizon about wines that he was proclaimed to be the dean of California winemaking, and he justly deserved it. . . . He [brought] to California not only the spirit of the high quality of wines and good taste, but [also] brought authority into winemaking." Louis P. Martini said that "André was a natural teacher. He loved to teach—he loved to get young people in there and, you know, just give them more and more information." Warren Winiarski observed, "Upon meeting [André], one was struck by this fantastic sense of authority and sureness and command of the materials that he possessed. And he spoke with such authority. It gave you such confidence to hear his answers that you began to think."[19]

Great teachers are also avid learners, and André never stopped learning from others as well. When Dick Peterson joined André at Beaulieu Vineyard in the late 1960s, Peterson said that Tchelistcheff "liked me telling him what the latest thinking was other than at BV. He was like a sponge. He soaked up anything that I could tell him." International wine consultant Chris Markell pointed out that André loved to mentor but "wasn't just there to give you the answers, either. André would say, 'What would you do in this situation? What do you think would be the best thing to do?' He might agree or not, but might say, 'Well, let's try it and see if it works.'" Winemaker Rick Sayre often told the story of André's return to Beaulieu in 1991 after eighteen years of post-retirement freelance consulting. Joel Aiken, BV's winemaker at that time, never worked with André prior to the former wine master's return. While walking side by side with Joel on a tour of BV's facilities, André expressed concern over the barrel-washing methods being used by Beaulieu's cellar workers. "This is the way you did it before," Joel reportedly said, "why should we change anything?" André replied, "Well, I've changed, the industry's changed, so why haven't you? There are better ways to wash the barrels."[20]

On December 7, 1991, family, friends, and national and international wine professionals feted André on his ninetieth birthday at San Francisco's Fairmont Hotel. One week after their five-star experience in San Francisco, André and Dorothy hosted a second birthday celebration in a downtown Napa restaurant. The Tchelistcheffs invited Beaulieu Vineyard's cellar and vineyard workers, none of whom had been asked to attend the exclusive Fairmont soiree. André's kind gesture on behalf of BV's laborers, in keeping with his democratic temperament, also reflected an empathetic spirit shaped no doubt from his earlier hardships. Adversity also forged Tchelistcheff's resiliency, enabling him to overcome challenge after challenge to eventually become one of America's most influential winemakers. Ironically, he had aspired to become a medical doctor, not an enologist, and in later years lamented what he described as his "primitiveness" and "limited field of knowledge." Tchelistcheff's self-deprecating assessment aside, revolutionary turmoil, exile, and familial responsibilities had forced André to abandon his earlier dream. "Anything that happens to me in my life, it just happens by necessity," André once mused.[21] The circumstances that necessitated his journey from the Old World to post-repeal California, one teeming with heartbreak, peril, and grit, began in a rural district situated one hundred miles southwest of Moscow during the twilight years of the tsarist Russian Empire.

CHAPTER 2

Kaluga

I never had the courage [to own a winery]. There were
offers; people with money who wanted to be my partners. But, remember, I am a child of the revolution. I
know what it means to lose everything overnight.

—ANDRÉ TCHELISTCHEFF

André Viktorovich Tchelistcheff's birth took place on November 24,
1901, according to imperial Russia's Julian calendar, although in later
years he always celebrated his birthday on December 7.[1] According to
family records, André's original forebear left Germany for Russia in
1237 and may have fought alongside Prince Alexander Nevsky in the
Battle of the Ice.[2] The first Tchelistcheff (pronounced CHEL-les-chef)
possessed a very large forehead, which translates as *tchelo* in Russian.
The Russian officers nicknamed André's distant ancestor Tchelo and
eventually called him Tchelishchij, or the "Great Forehead." Over the
centuries, Tchelishchij gradually morphed into Tchelistcheff. At the
time of his birth, André's father, Viktor, a highly respected jurist, also
served as an assistant professor at the University of Moscow. Eventually, André's father became the chief justice of the Court of Appeal
in imperial Russia as well as the president of the Imperial Jurists
Association. André's father was also an avid hunter and an exceptional
storyteller. In later years, he composed a number of fictional stories
based on his earlier experiences in rural Russia.[3]

13

In Viktor's narrative titled "Going to Mass," an uncle, who serves as a churchwarden, and his two nephews, Tikhon and Kolya, attempt to deliver candles to Sunday Mass at their local church. Outfitted in racoon pelisses, Circassian fur caps, and felt boots, the three set out in their horse-drawn sleigh across the snowy, forested plains of central Russia. As they neared the church, Kolya spotted a red fox, which provoked their uncle to hastily turn the sleigh around and race homeward to retrieve his wolfhounds. Once properly equipped with his dogs in tow, the three set out again, this time on a hunting expedition, and eventually encountered their prey. Suddenly finding itself in dire straits, the fox took off "like a red ribbon ... with its brush flying." Tikhon and Kolya jumped out of the sled, the hounds tumbled out after them, and the impulsive boys and yelping dogs gave chase. The uncle remained behind, trying to gain control of Strelka, his impressive Orloff horse, which bolted forward in a frenzied gallop. The uncle got his legs entangled in the reins, fell out of the sleigh, and was dragged along the snow while waving his arms and "cursing everything under the sun." When the uncle finally reached his nephews and baying hounds, he bawled, "Devils, fools, asses! ... Did you think the fox was going to wait for you?" Tikon and Kolya then directed his attention to the motionless fox lying in the snow, prompting their embarrassed uncle to exclaim, "Why didn't you say so?" Following their successful hunt, the three gathered their exhausted wolfhounds and returned home to clean up. Along the way, they heard the church bells peal, signaling the end of Sunday Mass. "What should we do about the candles?" Kolya asked his uncle. "What's the good of candles when the service is over?" his uncle replied.[4]

Viktor's wife and André's mother, Alexandra Yasinskaya, was a short, slender woman from whom André inherited his diminutive stature. Alexandra raised six children with Viktor, three daughters (Olga, Anne, and Alexandra) and three sons (André, Victor, and Nicolai). André's family owned a landed estate known as Novaya Derevnya in Borovsky district, Kaluga Oblast, located approximately a hundred miles southwest of Moscow. Novaya Derevnya originally encompassed nearly four thousand acres, but after Tsar Alexander II emancipated Russia's serfs in 1861, large portions of the estate were sold off to local peasants. The Tchelistcheffs farmed, bred Borzoi hunting dogs, and raised Orloff horses. The graceful Borzois, developed in Russia to track wolves and other predators, stood nearly thirty inches tall and weighed up to a hundred pounds. The Tchelistcheff hounds so impressed the American Teddy Roosevelt that he purchased two of them prior to World War I. In later years, one of André's most cherished possessions was his leather and horsehair hound whip, which was used to control or even save the dogs during hunting expeditions. The Tchelistcheff family's magnificent Orloffs, known for their speed and stamina, helped supply the imperial army with equestrian muscle.[5]

André's love for and curiosity about the natural world no doubt derived from his early childhood experiences on his family's rural estate. In the late imperial period, the Kaluga province encompassed forests of birch, oak, spruce, and pine; winding rivers; peasant villages; and expansive valleys. The birch tree, or *bereza*, is especially significant in Russian culture and is featured in music, poetry, and art. In Russian folklore, the birch often represents a slender, beautiful girl. It also symbolizes nature, protection, beauty, and spring. The folksong "Beriozka," which celebrates the birch tree, always brought André to tears.[6]

Summers in Kaluga were short, hot, and humid, and winters were long, cold, and snowy. In the depths of winter, hungry wolves scavenged the countryside and posed a constant threat. The mystique of Russia's rural expanses such as Kaluga captured the imagination of many of the empire's greatest nineteenth-century writers. The poet Alexander Pushkin, for example, once wrote, "Petersburg is our parlor, Moscow our maid's room, the countryside our study." Pushkin drew inspiration from his rural estate Mikhailovskoye, much as Leo Tolstoy did from his Yasnaya Polyana or Ivan Turgenev from his Spasskoye-Lyutovinovo. For these intellectuals, the Russian countryside, in all of its beauty, mystery, and paradoxes, constituted a life-giving force as well as a laboratory for social analysis.[7]

Since the Tchelistcheffs owned a substantial landed estate as well as a large townhome in Moscow, their family undoubtedly "ranked" in imperial Russia's complicated system of nobility. The family's several branches produced illustrious doctors, jurists, and teachers, as well as the neo-Romantic painter Pavel Tchelitchew, André's cousin. Nonetheless, André always downplayed any aristocratic pretensions within the Tchelistcheff clan. After becoming a naturalized U.S. citizen in 1945, André turned into an unwavering Democrat. In addition, he described his father as a progressive liberal who favored political and social reform. The senior Tchelistcheff as well as his eldest son likely eschewed the trappings of nobility and regarded imperial Russia's society of orders as an antiquated relic of the tsarist past. In fact, by the turn of the twentieth century, Russia's autocratic traditions faced mounting pressures for reform and, in some quarters, revolutionary transformation.[8]

André was born in an empire that straddled two continents and stretched six thousand miles west to east from Poland to the Pacific Ocean. Although the Great Russians constituted nearly half of Russia's population of approximately 170 million, its ethno-religious mosaic included Ukrainians, White Russians, Baltic and Volga Germans, Poles, Finns, Lithuanians, Letts, Estonians, Romanians, Armenians, Georgians, Turks, Mongols, and Jews. Russia's demographic heterogeneity and vast Euro-Asian topography generated a certain level of existential angst among Russia's intelligentsia and gave rise to polarizing debates between "Westernizers" and "Slavophiles" over their country's true identity. Compounding Russia's identity crisis were its repressive institutions of tsarist autocracy and religious orthodoxy, as well as its vast peasantry, largely illiterate and only several decades removed from serfdom. Because of their fundamental detachment from the government, organized religion, and the masses, many Russian intellectuals experienced a deep sense of alienation and embraced exaggerated notions of how to bring about historical change. Consequently, among the most alienated individuals, violent revolution seemed to be the only feasible option.[9]

André's birth also took place at a time of dramatic economic and social change. Bolstered by the reforms of Sergei Witte, who served as the finance minister in the tsarist government between 1892 and 1903, the Russian Empire lurched into the industrial age. Witte launched the construction of the Trans-Siberian Railway, promoted exports and the growth of heavy industry, encouraged foreign investment, and established a gold standard in Russia. By 1900 Russia's economy was growing at an annual rate of 8 percent. Industrial growth gave rise to an urban proletariat in the larger cities of European Russia, the Urals, and Ukraine, reaching a population of three million by the outbreak of World War I. As in the case of early industrialization elsewhere in Europe, working conditions were grueling and living accommodations appalling. Russia's autocratic government also banned labor unions, undermining a key component of workers' empowerment. Moreover, Russia's vast peasantry, at least three-quarters of the empire's population, remained rural, poor, and essentially powerless. "In the barren political soil of autocracy," writes historian Sean McMeekin, "it was not surprising that labor and peasant agitators, denied legal recourse or other means of redress, often resorted to violence."[10]

Russia's socioeconomic transformation at the turn of the twentieth century affected the intelligentsia as well, manifesting in the formation of national political movements for the first time in Russian history. The impetus for these political changes actually began during the reign of Tsar Alexander II (1855–81). He was known as the "Tsar Emancipator" for abolishing serfdom in 1861, yet he also provided limited governing powers to the middle and upper-middle classes through the creation of provincial councils known as zemstvo. In addition, Alexander II established the modern judiciary in Russia, a reform that directly benefited individuals such as André's father. By the late nineteenth century, economic development also expanded the ranks of the middle class, which desired additional liberal reforms. In 1905 moderate liberals established the political movement known as the Constitutional Democratic Party (whose adherents were known as Kadets); it sought to transform Russia into a constitutional monarchy or even a liberal republic. The historian Paul Miliukov, a close friend of André's father, cofounded and served as the first leader of the Kadets. When a national legislature (State Duma) was formed during the Revolution of 1905, the Kadets dominated it, thus demonstrating the potential for establishing a more liberal and democratic Russia. But as historian Nicholas Riasanovsky points out, "The [tsarist] government never accepted the liberal viewpoint, nor, of course, did the Russian radical and revolutionary movement accept it. The liberals thus had little opportunity to influence state policies or even to challenge them." As a result, "Russian liberalism never received its chance in imperial Russia."[11]

The major problem for Russian liberals was that the last two Romanov tsars, Alexander III (1881–94) and Nicholas II (1894–1917), resisted reform, tried to entrench autocracy, and sought to repress dissent with their political police and the military. Alexander III executed his autocratic power capably, but his son Nicholas II clearly did not. Nicholas, a weak and indecisive individual, relied on the advice of his wife, Alexandra. The tsarina Alexandra, German by origin, incited her husband to act as a pitiless autocrat and convinced Nicholas that the continuation of tsarist autocracy was God's will. Tragically, Alexandra also fell under the spell of a mysterious faith healer named Rasputin. Grigori Rasputin preached a doctrine he called "redemption through sin," believing that heavenly salvation came to those who drank alcohol excessively and practiced promiscuous sex. Rasputin also seemed to possess the power to cure the young tsarevich Alexei of his hemophilia. To the Romanov family, Rasputin was a man sent from heaven. As a result, the bizarre mystic managed to work his way into the inner ruling circle, even appointing and dismissing ministers when Nicholas left Petrograd (St. Petersburg) to command Russian troops at the front during World War I. The Rasputin scandal, combined with Russia's disastrous losses during the war, further eroded Nicholas's standing with the Russian masses. Even Rasputin's freakish murder in December 1916 could not save the imperial throne, which collapsed two months later in the February Revolution.[12]

Before its demise, tsarist autocracy succeeded in stifling liberalism but provided fertile soil for two revolutionary movements, the Socialist Revolutionaries and the Social Democrats. Founded in 1901, the Socialist Revolutionary Party evolved from the populist and nihilist movements of the nineteenth century. The Socialist Revolutionaries believed that the true revolutionary force in Russia sprang historically from the peasantry. They admired the Russian communal village (*mir*) and thought that it could serve as the basis of a socialist society. Unlike traditional Marxists, Socialist Revolutionaries did not believe that the urban proletariat represented the only revolutionary force, especially given its minuscule presence in Russia at the time. In contrast, the Social Democratic Party, founded in 1898, represented Russia's version of classical Marxian socialists who believed that the proletariat represented the foundation of a socialist revolution. Forced into exile by the tsarist political police (Okhrana) early on, the Social Democrats underwent a fateful split in 1903 into the Bolsheviks (majority) and Mensheviks (minority). The split was engineered by Vladimir Ulianov, also known as Lenin, who objected to the Menshevik view that a socialist party might encompass a wide variety of views. Lenin believed instead that a political party must consist of a small band of dedicated professional revolutionaries who would serve as the vanguard of the proletariat. In the words of one historian, Lenin "maintained that left to itself, the [proletariat] would do nothing. Hence the Russian Social Democrats must take power on behalf of the workers and rule in their name." In effect, Lenin's program was a "blueprint for dictatorship."[13]

Unquestionably, André grew up in an empire undergoing dramatic social, economic, and political change. During this transformation, Russian culture flourished, giving rise to world-class literature (Turgenev, Fyodor Dostoevsky, Tolstoy), theater (Anton Chekhov, Maxim Gorky, Nicholas Gogol), music (Peter Tchaikovsky, Modest Mussorgsky, Nicholas Rimsky-Korsakov), opera, and dance. André's family thrived in this cultural milieu and even possessed a private box at the Bolshoi Theatre in Moscow. Yet the most striking Russian reality was the deep chasm between "privileged" Russia and the masses. The stunning cultural achievements of this era largely bypassed the great majority of Russia's population. As one historian characterizes it, "Russia possessed . . . the best ballet in the world, but the majority of the people remained illiterate." André explained the cultural divide this way: "Culturally, intellectually, [Russians were] very ahead. We created great authors and great musicians, but in the average life, we were very retrograde."[14]

Socially André's family belonged to privileged Russia, but in the first four years of his life, André experienced life-threatening hardship. Until the age of five, André suffered from peritonitis, an inflammation of the membrane lining the inner wall of his abdomen. The condition, which causes acute abdominal pain, is deadly if left untreated. His parents feared the worst and did not expect their son to survive. André's father even traveled to the cathedral of Saint Nicholas in Bari, Italy, to pray for a miracle. At home, doctors drained fluid from André's abdomen on a weekly basis and placed him on an iron-rich diet, which included buckwheat kasha and bloody steaks. André found it difficult to eat or sleep and could only rest in the arms of his parents or his nurse. One of André's early memories was of his mother holding him in her arms in their Moscow townhome during the Revolution of 1905. She stood at the window to observe the street demonstrations, waiting anxiously for her brother-in-law to deliver provisions from the family estate. Suddenly, a bullet crashed through the window, passing between them. "It was very dangerous to [live and] travel in Moscow in 1905," André later observed.[15]

In many ways, the Revolution of 1905 served as a rehearsal for the upheavals of 1917. The crisis emanated from the contradictions inherent in Russia's dramatic socioeconomic transformation. Revolutions occur not when the masses are utterly destitute and oppressed, "but when there is growth, advancement, and high expectation, hampered, however, by an archaic and rigid established order." The revolutionary upheaval of 1905 was triggered on Sunday, January 22 (January 9 on the Russian calendar), in the Russian capital of St. Petersburg. Led by the radical Orthodox priest Georgy Gapon, 150,000 workers and their families marched to the Winter Palace to present a petition to Tsar Nicholas demanding an eight-hour workday, living wages, and the convocation of a Russian constituent assembly. Singing "God Save the Tsar," many held up icons and portraits of Nicholas II. Unbeknownst to the protestors, Nicholas spent the day in Tsarskoe Selo, the tsar's summer palace fifteen miles south of St. Petersburg. Upon reaching the Palace Square, the protestors encountered mounted Cossacks and police guards who panicked and began firing into the assembly, killing over two hundred men, women, and children, and wounding nearly eight hundred. The carnage, which became known as Bloody Sunday, sent shock waves throughout the empire. It prompted workers' strikes, peasant uprisings, mutinous rebellions in Russia's Black Sea fleet, and terrorist attacks against tsarist officials. A disastrous war against Japan in 1904–5 fueled the insurgency even further. In the Russo-Japanese War, Japan humiliated the Russians in the Battle at Mukden in February 1905 and virtually destroyed Russia's entire Baltic fleet in the Battle of Tsushima that May. The revolutionary turmoil also gave rise to a new institution called a workers' council (soviet) that sought to guide the radicalized masses. The St. Petersburg Soviet, led by the Menshevik (later Bolshevik) Lev Trotsky, helped direct a general strike in the fall of 1905 that virtually brought the empire to a standstill.[16]

Faced with an existential threat, Nicholas's finance minister Sergei Witte provided the tsar with two alternatives: appoint a military dictator to crush the revolution or convoke a representative State Duma (legislature) to divide Russia's liberals from the revolutionary socialists. Half measures, warned Witte, would be fatal. Nicholas chose the latter, promulgating the October Manifesto in 1905, which created a national legislature for the first time in Russian history. As Witte predicted, Russia's liberals seized the opportunity, with the Kadets dominating the first State Duma. Nicholas's bold action dampened the revolutionary fervor, the government disbanded the St. Petersburg Soviet, and, at least for the moment, the tsarist state remained intact. Rather than using the opportunity to build a legitimate constitutional monarchy, however, the tsar quickly reverted to his autocratic proclivities. Most notably, in May 1906 Nicholas issued the Fundamental Laws, which empowered the tsar with complete control of the executive, the armed forces, the nation's foreign policy, and the Orthodox Church, and gave him veto power over all Duma legislation and the right to retain the title of "autocrat." "The tsar's insistent attachment to this increasingly archaic political vision," according to historical scholars, "ultimately became a source of dangerous instability in the emerging political order of late imperial Russia."[17]

In the decade following the Revolution of 1905, André Tchelistcheff recovered his strength and received home tutoring at his family's country estate to prepare him for high school in Moscow. André later recalled sitting at the breakfast table with his father, who listened as André to read the newspaper aloud to him. During these occasions, André's father explained the meanings of the words, the nature of the problems, and the nuances of the political and constitutional terminology. André surmised that his father devoted such tremendous effort to his son's education because André was the eldest boy and his "life was kind of a miracle in the family." André also studied mathematics, languages, and literature; learned to love music and opera; and experienced the thrill of travel. At the age of eleven, he passed the high school entrance examination and for the next six years attended a lycée in Moscow. André lived in his family's Moscow home, built by his grandfather and designed by his uncle, located on Nicolo Peskovsky Lane near Spaso Peskovsky Square. The young Tchelistcheff served as an altar boy in the Russian Orthodox Church located on the square. André was on track to graduate in the spring of 1918 and aspired to attend the University of Moscow to study medicine. Revolutionary turmoil in the fall of 1917, however, upended his high school career and dramatically changed the course of his life.[18]

Historians continue to debate the "inevitability" of a revolution in 1917. Between 1906 and the outbreak of World War I in August 1914, Russia remained a paradox, experiencing significant spurts of economic growth mixed with substantial doses of political repression. In 1906 Nicholas appointed Petr Stolypin prime minister. Alongside Witte, Stolypin stood as one of the most gifted bureaucrats of the era. To quell internal unrest, Stolypin set up special courts-martial to root out sedition and dispatch convicted dissidents to prison, exile, and the gallows. So many of the accused were hanged in 1906 that contemporaries referred to the noose as "Stolypin's necktie." Meanwhile, Stolypin implemented significant land reforms that were designed to incentivize peasants to relinquish their communes for private holdings. The results were dramatic: nearly one-fifth of the European Russian peasantry abandoned their communal strips, resulting in much higher agricultural productivity and an export surplus of twenty million tons of grain by 1913. Stolypin warned, however, that Russia needed twenty more years of peace to successfully complete its economic transition. "War during the next years," he advised, "especially for reasons the people will not understand, would be fatal for Russia and for the dynasty." Stolypin never witnessed the consequences of his prophecy because Russia's talented statesman fell to an assassin's bullet in September 1913.[19]

The following year, another assassin's attack in Sarajevo, Bosnia-Herzegovina, killed the heir to the Austrian throne, Franz Ferdinand, and his wife, Sophie, and provoked a monthlong diplomatic crisis in July 1914 that drew Russia into the kind of conflict that Stolypin most feared. As tensions mounted throughout Europe that month, all of Nicholas II's advisers pressured him to order a general mobilization of Russian troops to prepare for war against Germany and Austria-Hungary. At first Nicholas balked. On July 29 he told an aide that "everything possible must be done to save the peace. I will not become responsible for a monstrous slaughter." Yet the next day Nicholas relented, and by August 1, Russia was at war against its imperial rivals. From its inception, World War I proved to be a disaster for imperial Russia. Within five months, the fighting killed 400,000 men and left a million wounded. By mid-1915, one quarter of all troops dispatched to the front were herded into battle unarmed, magnifying the senseless slaughter and the social chasm between ordinary soldiers and their commanding officers. Compounding wartime troop attrition, the conflict strained Russia's economy to the breaking point, resulting in food shortages and rising prices. In major cities such as St. Petersburg (renamed Petrograd at the outset of the war for patriotic reasons), people—mainly the women left behind—scavenged for food and turned to prostitution and crime to survive. On top of all of these sacrifices, the Russians endured a government being run by Nicholas's narrow-minded, German-born wife and the mystical charlatan Rasputin.[20]

On February 23, 1917 (March 8 on the Gregorian calendar), thousands of women textile workers in Petrograd walked out of their factories to protest the severe bread shortages. Other disgruntled workers and students joined them in street demonstrations, demanding an end to the war and the abolition of autocracy. Two days later, the empress Alexandra wrote to Nicholas denouncing the "hooligan movement" of "young boys and girls running about and screaming that they have no bread." She mockingly observed, "If it were very cold they would probably stay indoors." Nicholas responded by ordering the commander of the Petrograd military district to quell the disturbances, but the dispatched troops fraternized with the protestors instead. On February 27, members of the Duma formed the Russian Provisional Government, dominated at first by the Kadets. Finally accepting the only rational choice, Tsar Nicholas abdicated his throne on March 2 (15), thus ending three hundred years of Romanov rule. The February Revolution seemed to represent a new stage in Russia's political history, but the outcome was far from definitive. From the outset, the provisional government faced the monumental challenges of managing an unpopular war, a struggling economy, and a rebellious peasantry. Furthermore, the fledgling republic found itself in competition with a socialist rival, the Petrograd Soviet. Who was in charge?[21]

Lenin, the Bolshevik leader, was now convinced that the February Revolution created the conditions for a socialist revolutionary takeover. Still in exile in early 1917, Lenin's vehement opposition to what he regarded as an imperialist-capitalist war as well as his fanatical commitment to revolution at any price impressed Germany. As a result, the German Foreign Office decided to facilitate Lenin's return to Russia by transporting him by train through German territory. Germany regarded Lenin as "the critical catalyst of chaos, a one-man demolition crew sent to wreck Russia's war effort." Arriving at Petrograd's Finland Station on April 3 (16), 1917, Lenin soon released his "April Theses," which promised peace, land, bread, and "all power to the soviets." During the remainder of 1917, Lenin, with substantial financial assistance from Germany, concentrated on sowing Bolshevik propaganda and in gaining control of the various soviets that had sprouted up throughout Russia. In July 1917, the Bolsheviks launched a premature coup in the wake of a disastrous military offensive devised by Alexander Kerensky, now prime minister of the Russian Provisional Government. By September 1917, however, Kerensky's precarious hold on power weakened significantly following Gen. Lavr Kornilov's apparent military coup and attempt to restore order in the Russian capital. Kerensky's final collapse came on October 25 (November 7) when the Bolsheviks seized telephone exchanges, railway stations, and electric power plants in Petrograd. The October Revolution, which replaced a liberal republic with a ruthless dictatorship, ushered in a new era of repression. "To hold onto state power and to destroy their [class] enemies, the Bolshevik leaders were explicit about their readiness to use the most 'draconian measures' (Lenin's words), including mass arrests, summary executions, and terror."[22]

When the Bolshevik takeover appeared imminent, Kerensky contacted André's father to warn him of the danger. Viktor's friend Paul Miliukov, the Kadet leader who served as minister of foreign affairs in the Russian Provisional Government's first cabinet, had offered Viktor an important position in the Department of Justice. Tchelistcheff's link to the provisional government, combined with his former position as chief justice of the Court of Appeal in the imperial bureaucracy, made him a class enemy subject to arrest and even execution. Kerensky himself fled in disguise on the morning of October 25. Other government ministers barricaded themselves inside the Winter Palace in Petrograd. The new Bolshevik government quickly established the Extraordinary Commission to Combat Counterrevolution, Sabotage, and Speculation (Cheka), which dedicated itself to rooting out class enemies and eliminating them. Felix Dzerzhinsky, leader of the Cheka, proclaimed that his organization stood for organized terror. "This should be frankly admitted," he said. "Terror is an absolute necessity during times of revolution. . . . Do not think that I seek forms of revolutionary justice; we are not in need of justice now." In these extreme circumstances, Viktor Tchelistcheff was branded an outlaw and forced to travel underground. According to André, immediately following the October Revolution, his father "never was able to spend one single night with the family."[23]

For the time being, André's family traveled between Moscow and his uncle's estate in Kaluga province. Bolshevik partisans had already destroyed André's neighboring family home. Its destruction happened on a day when André and his sister Alexandra were checking on the livestock at their original family estate. Local villagers suddenly arrived to warn the Tchelistcheff children about the imminent arrival of Red partisans, who were no doubt galvanized by Lenin's directive to "expropriate the expropriators." André and his sister wisely fled. The Bolshevik militia let loose a reign of terror upon their arrival at André's boyhood home. The intruders torched the rural estate, which housed Grandfather Tchelistcheff's exclusive library, and confiscated the Orloff horses. Attacking anything that stood out as a symbol of privilege, the Bolshevik militia also rounded up the Borzoi hunting dogs and completed their vengeful orgy by hanging every one of the wolfhounds. "These were awful days," André reflected, "days of fires and destruction, terror and blood." Soon after these tragic events, the political commissar from the nearest town visited the Tchelistcheffs at their uncle's estate. After informing them that the government was confiscating the property, the commissar gave the Tchelistcheffs twenty-four hours to move out. He also ordered them to take along no more than two changes of clothes. The next morning André's family made its way to the local railway station for a final trip to Moscow.[24]

Although "Moscow was still boiling," as André characterized it, his family resided in its home in the city for several more months. A political committee elected by the neighborhood community protected their property for the time being, but expropriation loomed. The terror being directed against "class enemies," one historian observes, "prompted an unprecedented flight of the brightest and best in Russian society. . . . Their homes were confiscated, their furniture seized and their clothes requisitioned for the state. . . . Of those intellectuals, scientists and artists who had not been mown down by the Cheka, between one and two million fled abroad." In the summer of 1918, André's father slipped out of Russia to join the White Army in the south. The Tchelistcheff family—including André, his mother, his three sisters, two brothers, and his grandparents—decided to join Viktor. They fled Moscow by train in October.[25]

As the train passed through the rural Russian countryside, André reflected on the happy times spent on his family estate. He thought about the breakfast conversations with his father and the intellectual stimulation they had provided. André recalled hunting alongside his father and grandfather, accompanied by the elegant Borzoi wolfhounds. He remembered the fragrant cherry orchards, the dairy cattle, and the horse and buggies traversing Kaluga's dirt roads to deliver cream, butter, and milk to the Moscow market. Also deeply etched in André's memory were the joyous Russian Easter celebrations when his grandmother fattened turkeys on walnut meat for the holiday meal. In later years, André likened his family's exodus to Yuri Zhivago's train journey through the Urals to Varykino in David Lean's epic film *Doctor Zhivago*. Every time André watched *Doctor Zhivago*, he wept, Dorothy said.

"That was the last day that I saw everything that was so close to my heart," André recalled, "and I haven't been able to return." Meanwhile, the Russian Civil War, pitting the Bolshevik Red Army against the loosely allied White Army, had already begun.[26]

At the time the Tchelistcheffs fled Russia, the Bolsheviks found themselves in precarious circumstances. Russia's major cities faced food shortages so severe that the government deployed "food procurement brigades" to the countryside to requisition grain from the peasantry. Earlier in 1918, the Bolshevik government signed the Treaty of Brest-Litovsk with Germany, pulling Russia out of World War I at a very steep price. Russia conceded the independence or German control of Ukraine, Poland, Belarus, Finland, Lithuania, Latvia, and Estonia—almost the entire western portion of the Russian Empire. In effect, Russia lost a quarter of its arable land, 40 percent of its population, a third of its manufacturing industries, and three-quarters of its coalfields. The economic implosion and humiliating peace terms alienated groups on the left as well as the right. Fanny Kaplan, a Socialist Revolutionary, shot Lenin at close range in August 1918, nearly killing him. For the most part, however, the Whites drew their support from army officers, Cossacks, and the social classes overthrown in the October Revolution. They also received limited support with troops and war matériel from Britain, France, and the United States. In the east, the Siberian People's Army was led by Adm. Alexander Kolchak and reinforced by fifty thousand Czechoslovakian prisoners of war. In the northwest, Gen. Nikolai Yudenich organized a Northwestern Army faction in Estonia. Viktor Tchelistcheff decided to join General Kornilov's White Volunteer Army in Ukraine that was supported by Gen. Petr Krasnov's Don Cossacks.[27]

André's father faced several obstacles in getting his family out of Russia and into Ukraine. First, until its defeat in World War I, Germany occupied Ukraine. Second, to leave Russia, the Tchelistcheffs needed official documentation from the Bolshevik/Soviet government. André's father solved the second problem by obtaining fictitious passports from a Soviet official whom Viktor had saved during the 1905 Revolution. Viktor's friend also happened to be a close associate of Trotsky, one of the most important Bolshevik leaders next to Lenin. The next problem, crossing the border into Ukraine, was equally daunting. When the Tchelistcheffs arrived at the border, André's uncle and his family, as well as several other family friends, joined the evacuees. "For a great amount of money," according to André, his father secured a guide who led the exiles through a forest and toward a German outpost. When they arrived at the checkpoint, the Tchelistcheffs surrendered their false passports while surreptitiously retaining their official documentation in their shoes. André's mother and uncle (her twin brother) spoke fluent German to the guards, André recalled; so after two hours of interrogation, the Germans "allowed us to proceed."[28]

The Tchelistcheffs traveled to Gomel, a Ukrainian town along the Dnieper River in the Pale of Jewish Settlement. After experiencing severe food shortages and witnessing the mass starvation taking place in central Russia, Gomel seemed a godsend. Businesses in the Jewish community flourished under German occupation. "All stores were open," André observed, with "bread, meat, sausages—everything was just unbelievable." Following their brief stay in Gomel, the Tchelist-cheffs boarded a boat for Kyiv, where the family benefited immensely from Viktor's network of political connections. André's father was appointed secretary of justice in the White government for the duration of the civil war. The family then moved to Novorossiysk, a major port city on the Black Sea. "I was seventeen years of age," André observed, "already a young man, and my dream, of course, was immediately to join the White Army." Reluctantly, Viktor reached out to Gen. Anton Denikin ("what am I going to do with my son André?") and learned about a new branch of the Military Academy of Kyiv opening in Ekaterinodar. André enrolled in the officer's course, earned a degree as a second lieutenant, and in 1919 joined Denikin's White Army group in the Crimean Peninsula.[29]

In the year André joined Denikin's Volunteer Army, two of the three major White Army factions experienced temporary success and ultimate failure in their conflict with the Bolshevik Red Army. Under the leadership of Trotsky, the Red Army had five million conscripts and seventy-five thousand officers by 1919. Trotsky recruited most of the officers from the ranks of the former imperial army. He earned the men's support by flanking them with political commissars and making clear that their loyalty was tantamount to their family's survival. Trotsky's centralized command structure also provided the Reds with a clear advantage over the White Army, which struggled with inadequate coordination, divided leadership, limited supplies, and poor communication. Nonetheless, the fortunes of Admiral Kolchak's Siberian People's Army and General Yudenich's Northwestern Army appeared most promising in the spring of 1919. The previous November Kolchak assumed the title of supreme ruler of the new Provisional All-Russian Government based in the temporary capital of Omsk. In a spring offensive, Kolchak's forces pushed as far as the Volga River with their sights set on linking with British troops in Archangel; however, a Red Army counteroffensive in the summer of 1919 pushed Kolchak's army back to the Urals. By October the Reds crossed the Ishim River, the last natural barrier before Omsk. Refugees streamed into Omsk in front of the approaching Red Army. An eyewitness described the scene: "Peasants had deserted their fields, students their books, doctors their hospitals, scientists their laboratories, workmen their workshops. . . . We were being swept away in the wreckage of a demoralized army." The Czechoslovak Legion, Kolchak's former ally, captured him in November and ransomed the supreme ruler to Bolshevik partisans in Irkutsk. Following an abbreviated "trial," Kolchak was executed in February 1920.[30]

Yudenich's position appeared equally promising in the spring of 1919, only to collapse by the end of the year. In May Yudenich's White Northwestern Army captured the Russian city of Pskov, less than two hundred miles from Petrograd. At this point, Yudenich tried but failed to win military support from the White Finns and Estonians, and he ignored Britain's demand that he transfer his forces to Denikin's front. Instead, the Northwestern Army set out on its own to assault Petrograd and achieved remarkable early success. Yudenich's troops moved rapidly through Pavlovsk and Tsarskoe Selo, and into Pulkovo, only fifteen miles from the former Russian capital.[31] In response to the crisis, Trotsky traveled to Pulkovo in his armored train car, mounted a horse to personally address his troops, and in a fiery speech rallied them to defend to the death the "capital of the revolution." Bolstered by troop reinforcements from Petrograd that flooded into Pulkovo, the Red Army forced Yudenich's army to retreat all the way to Estonia. Although Trotsky chose not to pursue him, Yudenich and the Northwestern Army were finished.[32]

André joined the third and most skillful major White Army faction, Denikin's Volunteer Army. By the beginning of 1919, Denikin had assembled a force numbering 117,000 men. Denikin also gained the temporary support of sixty-five thousand troops from a French expeditionary force that had landed on the Crimean Peninsula in December 1918. The French forces, consisting primarily of Greek, Romanian, and French colonial troops, showed little enthusiasm for fighting and evacuated the Crimea in April 1919. Despite this setback, the departure of German troops from Russian territory under the terms of the armistice ending World War I provided Denikin with freedom of movement in Ukraine. In early July 1919, Denikin issued a Moscow Directive, an ambitious goal of occupying the Soviet capital before the onset of winter. Beginning that month, the Volunteer Army moved north into the heart of Ukraine. Withstanding Red Army counterattacks in August and September, Denikin continued to push north. By mid-October, the Volunteer Army seized Orel, a Russian city only 250 miles from Moscow. Denikin's forces now controlled 350,000 square miles of territory and a population of 42 million people. On Denikin's right flank, Baron Petr Wrangel's Caucasus Army had already seized Tsaritsyn. The Bolsheviks faced an existential threat from the south.[33]

Despite Denikin's remarkable advance, his army encountered several insurmountable problems. By October 1919, the Volunteer Army was 400 miles north of the nearest supply depot, crippling Denikin's momentum. Wrangel, who succeeded Denikin in early 1920, regarded the Moscow Directive as "the death sentence of the South Russian armies." He said, "Striving for space, we endlessly stretched ourselves into a spider web, and wanting to hold on to everything and to be *everywhere* strong were everywhere weak." A second and related problem concerned the Volunteer Army's lack of supplies. As a result of shortages, it relied on self-supply, requisitioning food, medicine, and weaponry from local peasants. This practice alienated the Russian locals, prompting peasants to refer to Denikin's troops as the Looter Army. Finally, the Red Army rallied in late October 1919 and began to push Denikin's forces southward. Between October and early January, the Volunteer Army retreated 450 miles through, as Wrangel characterized it, "places where the population had learned to hate it." Chased by Red Army cavalry, Denikin's troop strength fell by half by December 1919.[34]

Early that month, Denikin moved Wrangel from the Caucasus Army to the Volunteer Army, but the setbacks continued. Kyiv fell in mid-December, Tsaritsyn in early January. When it crossed the Don River on January 7, the Volunteer Army had lost everything that had been captured in 1919. When Ekaterinodar fell in March, the British provided ships to transport the remaining White troops to their last sanctuary, the Crimean Peninsula. The Crimea is virtually an island protected from the mainland by the defensible Perekop Isthmus. At this point realizing he was finished, Denikin relinquished his command to Wrangel and sailed off into exile. Wrangel, who rather remarkably attained the rank of major general at the age of thirty-nine, proceeded to assemble a force of thirty thousand frontline soldiers supplemented by a considerable number of refugee Don Cossacks. Wrangel believed that one of Denikin's key failures was in losing the support of the local population. As he once said, the Whites needed "to make leftist policies with rightist hands." He also changed the name of his army from "Volunteer" to "Russian," a symbolic gesture to raise the stakes of his mission. With his revitalized forces, Wrangel pushed beyond the Perekop Isthmus between June and October to secure the rich agricultural territory to the north. By November 1920, however, Wrangel's forces began to melt against the Red Army's overwhelming numerical superiority. White Army survival, Wrangel now realized, depended on the evacuation of his beleaguered troops.[35]

In the last weeks of their struggle against the Reds on the Crimean Peninsula, André Tchelistcheff's White Army unit came under withering fire during its assault on a Red Army machine-gun emplacement. Unlike most of his comrades, André survived but just barely. He withdrew from the battlefield and quickly became disoriented in the freezing, whiteout conditions. André then decided to crawl into a thicket and lie hidden from the enemy, only to gradually lose consciousness. When news of the battlefield disaster reached André's family, then residing in Yalta, they conducted a Russian Orthodox funeral service for their supposedly fallen son. On that same day, a Cossack detail arrived to collect the battlefield dead, spotted André's seemingly lifeless body, and tossed it atop one of its horses. Much to the Cossacks' amazement, they quickly discovered that André was in fact alive but suffering from severe frostbite and hypothermia. The Cossack horsemen transported him to a nursing station, where André began his miraculous recovery. The nurses saved André's frostbitten legs by soaking them in olive oil for nearly two months. Amazingly, André's leg strength returned and endured. Years later, even in his early nineties, he could still "outwalk the boys in the vineyard."[36]

Beginning on November 14, 1920, French and British ships evacuated 146,000 White Army troops and civilians from Sevastopol to Constantinople (Istanbul), 350 miles away. From the outset, Wrangel's campaign was doomed to failure. With the collapse of the Northwestern and Siberian People's Armies, Wrangel stood little chance of prevailing over the Red Army. In addition to their insufficient battlefield coordination, the White armies lacked a common vision beyond the principle of anti-Bolshevism. Furthermore, the Whites failed to win over the Russian population. Regardless of political outlook, White leaders generally rejected the outright seizure of estate lands that the peasants had carried out during the revolution. If restored to power, the White leadership made clear that Russia would return to the rule of law and the sanctity of private property. As a result, "whereas the upper and middle classes generally favored the Whites, and the vast majority of workers backed the Reds, the peasants, the great majority of the people, tended to support neither side enthusiastically but were likely to be more hostile to the Whites." Of all the White leaders, Wrangel understood this predicament the best. He later referred to his Crimean campaign as the "epilogue of the Russian tragedy." For André Tchelistcheff, the Russian tragedy that began with his family's dispossession and nearly ended with his own battlefield death set the stage for a new ordeal—eighteen years of European exile.[37]

CHAPTER 3

The Apache Dancer

Anything that happens to me in my life, it just
happens by necessity.

—ANDRÉ TCHELISTCHEFF

André's cultured background, combined with his two near-death
experiences, prepared him well for his next ordeal. Following their
evacuation from Crimea in late 1920, the White Army troops remained
anchored outside Constantinople for weeks. "That was the most tragical
days of our life," André said, "because we didn't have any supplies." To
avoid starvation, soldiers exchanged their wristwatches and wedding
rings for bread and figs with the thousands of Turkish and Greek
merchants in their small boats surrounding the Russian flotilla. When
orders to disembark finally came, the regular Russian troops were
dispatched to an internment camp in Gallipoli, while the Allies sent
the Cossack irregulars to the island of Lemnos in the Aegean Sea. For
the next fifteen months, the regular Russian forces remained in the
Gallipoli camp, subsisting on Allied supplies and guarded by French
colonial troops. "We were retrained there and kept as a military unit
with the idea that the Allies will send [us] back to Russia," André said.
At the time, André fully believed that the Bolshevik regime would
collapse within a year or two. Eventually, however, it became increasingly clear to the western Allies and to André "that the White action
of Russia is beaten." André's regiment abandoned the Gallipoli camp

in 1922 and set off for its next assignment, hard labor in the coal mines outside Gorna-Dzhumaya, Bulgaria.[1]

Bulgaria allied with the Central Powers in the First World War and therefore represented one of the defeated powers in the war's aftermath. The settlement imposed on Bulgaria by the Paris Peace Conference—territorial loss, reparations, and a reduction in armed forces—though not crippling, provoked humiliation and resentment among many Bulgarian nationalists and discredited Bulgaria's wartime regime. King Ferdinand abdicated in favor of his son Boris III, and a new political party, the Agrarian Party, came to power. Led by Aleksandr Stamboliyski, the Agrarian Party introduced a progressive income tax, the expansion of public education, and land reforms directed against the country's large estates. The peasantry embraced Stamboliyski's land reforms, but many property owners viewed them as a major step toward communism. In the summer of 1923, the Bulgarian middle class, the military, and the king turned against Stamboliyski's government and overthrew it in a military coup. Stamboliyski was captured, tortured, and killed. On the eve of the coup, Bulgarian military officials recalled André's regiment from its labor camps to participate in the overthrow, providing it with weapons and ammunition. "We restored the order and saved Bulgaria from the communist revolution," André said. In fact, the Bulgarian Communists declared their neutrality at the outset of the 1923 coup and were crushed in their own coup attempt two years later. The overthrow of Stamboliyski's democratically elected government paved the way instead for a right-wing dictatorship under Aleksandr Tsankov.[2]

Following André's service in Bulgaria, his regiment relocated to the Yugoslav-Italian border to guard the frontier on behalf of the Yugoslavian king Alexander. Soon thereafter André's regimental commander announced that any Russian exile who possessed a diploma or partial diploma had "the right to register for further education." André qualified with his documentation from the Military Academy of Kyiv. "We were called up regiment by regiment," André said, to meet with a representative of the Nansen Committee. In 1920 the League

of Nations council appointed the Norwegian oceanographer Fridtjof
Nansen the high commissioner responsible for the protection of a half
million Russian refugees. Ultimately, Nansen wanted to repatriate
the Russians. In the meantime, he needed to secure their legal status,
facilitate their emigration to other countries, and help them build
productive and sustainable lives. One of Nansen's key solutions for
displaced persons was an identification card known thereafter as the
"Nansen passport," which allowed refugees to travel freely throughout
much of Europe and legally protected them from deportation. In 1922
Nansen won the Nobel Peace Prize for his farsighted humanitarian
initiative. For Russian exiles such as André, the Nansen passport
represented a godsend, especially after Lenin revoked the citizenship
of all Russian expatriates on December 15, 1921.[3]

The Nansen representative who addressed André's regiment spoke
in French, German, and English but not Russian. Fortunately, André
spoke fluent French and possessed reasonable proficiency in German.
The Nansen official told André's regiment that each Russian émigré
deserved access to further education. "Russia needs to be restored to
a liberal democracy," he said, "and will need your brains." All of the
Russians applauded. André's regiment also learned that due to the
limited number of scholarships, diploma holders received first priority
for college assignments. Those possessing partial diplomas, such as
André, needed retraining to pass a college entrance examination. Soon
thereafter, André set off for Mährisch Trübau, Czechoslovakia, to begin
his training program. André and his cohort of seasoned veterans found
the training difficult. Nonetheless, "we managed it," he said, "and we
passed the final exam in Czechoslovakian." The successful matriculants
then drew lots for their college placement. André got assigned to the
Institute of Agricultural Technology in Brno, Czechoslovakia. "I did
not like my assignment," he said, "because I still dreamt of becoming
a medical doctor."[4]

Among the new states to emerge in interwar eastern Europe,
Czechoslovakia maintained a functional democracy throughout

this period. Its interwar political stability owes a great deal to the leadership of Tomáš Masaryk. A philosophy professor and political activist, Masaryk organized a Czech military force in support of the western Allies in the First World War. Simultaneously, Masaryk formed a committee that lobbied for Czech independence. By the time of the postwar settlement, the Allies recognized his committee as the provisional government of an independent Czechoslovakia. Masaryk went on to become the republic's first president. Reelected three more times, he succeeded in uniting the various nationalities in the region, including the Czechs, Slovaks, Ruthenians, and Germans. As in Bulgaria, Masaryk's government moved quickly to dismember large landed estates. In addition, his party promoted the development of the country's modern brewing and textile industries. Masaryk also worked tirelessly to promote fairness toward all sections of Czechoslovakia's diverse population and, as a result, enjoyed immense respect and support. Despite Czechoslovakia's track record of political stability, ethnic harmony evaporated quickly in the late 1930s. Nazi Germany's deliberate attempt to stimulate and support German nationalism in Czechoslovakia's Sudetenland region posed an existential threat to the country's democratic experiment.[5]

André benefitted from Czechoslovakia's relative stability in the first decade after the Great War, spending two productive years in Brno between 1927 and 1929. Aside from André's mother, the rest of André's family flourished during this period as well. André's father, Viktor, worked as a consultant to the Ministry of Justice in Belgrade, Yugoslavia. His sister Alexandra enrolled in the Sorbonne in Paris, joining thousands of other Russian émigrés in the French capital, and graduated with a degree in pharmacy. André's other sisters, Olga and Anne, lived with Viktor, taking care of their father after their mother, Alexandra, died of tuberculosis at the age of forty-two. André's younger brother Victor graduated with a degree in architecture from the University of Prague, and his youngest brother, Nicolai, studied at Belgium's University of Louvain, obtaining his degree in civil engineering and architecture. Meanwhile, André took classes at the Institute of Agricultural Technology in Brno, a comprehensive educational experience that transformed his life. "My knowledge of physiology, my knowledge of zoology, my knowledge of general agricultural science, agricultural engineering, my knowledge of chemistry and physics, was the basis of my success in my career," he said. André later recalled completing a final examination in animal physiology from an "unbelievably" difficult professor at Brno. The professor said, "Mr. Tchelistcheff, you deserve an 'A+' for your outstanding performance." Nevertheless, since "only God has a hundred percent of knowledge," he added, "and because even I do not have an 'A,' I give you a 'B+!'" Part of André's coursework also included six months of field training in the Tokaj region of Hungary, his first working experience with viticulture. André completed his degree in engineering agronomy in 1929 and started his career as an agronomist in the experimental station in Dubrovnik, Yugoslavia, his second exposure to viticulture.[6]

In 1930 André also married Catherine Alexandruna Perelmoff, the daughter of another Russian expatriate family. Catherine grew up in Buryatia, a region in the Russian Far East that is adjacent to the eastern shores of Lake Baikal. Prior to the October Revolution, Catherine's father practiced law, served as a judge, and traded gold for a living. After the Bolshevik takeover, the relatively wealthy Perelmoffs became class enemies of the regime and, like the Tchelistcheffs, were forced into exile. According to André, the family initially emigrated to Shanghai, China, joining a substantial Russian exile community there, before moving to Yugoslavia in the late 1920s. Eventually, the Perelmoffs settled in the United States.[7]

One year after André's marriage to Catherine, following the couple's move first to Belgrade and then to France, Catherine gave birth to Dimitri, André's only child. In 1931 André entered into a partnership with Prince Troubetskoy, an émigré Russian nobleman who owned a property a hundred miles southwest of Paris. With Troubetskoy's support, André began raising poultry and harvesting grain in Seine-et-Oise,

France's largest, richest agricultural region. At the time, André's career interest focused on animal production rather than viticulture. "I was far more interested in animal husbandry," he said. "I took this as a security." He published a book on poultry production, with editions in both Russian and French, and taught part-time in a local agricultural training school. In 1933 André's animal husbandry career, on such a promising trajectory, met with catastrophe. "We lost everything in a hailstorm," he said. The egg-sized hail "even killed the calves." The partnership ended, the property sold, and André moved his family temporarily to a poultry farm in Bonny-sur-Loire. Once again, tragedy struck. André's wife, Catherine, began to experience severe back pain and even lost her ability to walk for a time. With her sister's support, Catherine, along with her son, Dimitri, traveled to the United States for medical treatment in 1936 and did not return to Paris until early 1938. A spinal tumor, physicians discovered, was the source of Catherine's debilitating pain. As crises mounted, André elected to start a new career. "I decided to retrain in viticulture and enology," André said. He then left for Paris and entered a postgraduate training program at the Institute of National Agronomy.[8]

André's career shift toward winemaking was not purely accidental; wine figured prominently in his childhood experiences. On André's first birthday, his godfather, Alexander Kotlyarov, bequeathed to the young Tchelistcheff a vineyard in Crimea. Family dinners often featured bottles of Bordeaux or Vouvray, and decanters of Madeira and port always graced the Tchelistcheffs' living room table. "It was absolutely normal to have wine on the table, and we were trained by our father to understand the wine," André said. During André's European exile, he also studied winemaking in the Tokaj region as well as at the experimental station in Dubrovnik prior to moving to France. In effect, André decided to use his broad training in agronomy, seasoned by his viticultural experiences in eastern Europe, as a bridge toward a career as a professional viticulturist and enologist. Since he now resided in interwar France, why not learn from the finest wine experts in the world?[9]

France's winemaking prowess dates back to the sixth century BCE. The Etruscans, a pre-Roman civilization in central Italy, began shipping wine to southern France around this time. Soon, however, the local French inhabitants began importing Etruscan grapevines and producing their own wine. Later in the first millennium BCE, the Romans expanded their empire into Gaul and, once established, spread viticulture into Burgundy, Bordeaux, and the Rhône Valley. The Romans also imported new varieties of vines and introduced innovations in winemaking as France, along with Germany and Spain, became centers of the European wine industry. With the collapse of Rome's imperial unity in the fifth century CE, the French wine trade stagnated, and vineyard production fell under the control of the Catholic Church. The Carolingians revived the wine trade in the eighth century, and by the late Middle Ages, wine had once again become France's most important export. In fact, one of the most significant advances in the history of wine occurred in medieval Burgundy.

Founded in 1098, the Cistercian order of Burgundian monks tended their crops and especially their grapevines with fastidious zeal. Early on the Cistercians learned that specific locales mattered significantly in the production of great wines. Year after year, they recorded which plots of land produced healthy grapes, noted where bud break came early or late, and observed where fruit ripened early or irregularly. Most important, the Cistercians also discovered that the choice of grape mattered as much as the locale. While the Cistercians were not unique in their devotion to vineyard management, "they were the first to care about their terroirs."[10] Terroir, a French term with no exact English translation, constitutes the sum total of every environmental force affecting a vineyard site: soil, slope, elevation, rainfall, temperature, wind velocity, and orientation to the sun. Site-specific vineyards, planted with the most appropriate grape varietals, provided the foundation for the greatest winemaking feats of the future.[11]

As the Cistercian example suggests, the church played a central role in the development of France's wine industry right up until the era of the French Revolution. During the rule of Napoleon Bonaparte, the French government secularized vineyard ownership. No longer the monopoly of thousands of monks, wine production nonetheless continued to flourish in France during much of the nineteenth century. Two additional innovations during this period—one scientific and the other cultural—solidified France's position as the epicenter of the wine world.

One of the most important advances in the history of winemaking, with France once again in the forefront, originated in the analysis of wine's chemical composition. In 1860 the French chemist and microbiologist Louis Pasteur, who directed the School of Scientific Studies at the École Normale Supérieure in Paris, explained for the first time what happens during the process of wine's fermentation. Pasteur's chemical research demonstrated that living yeasts serve as catalysts for the transformation of grape juice into wine and that this transformation only continues with the ongoing engagement of these same yeasts. His scientific fame as an analyst of the microbiology of fermentation as well as disease culminated in the foundation of the Pasteur Institute in Paris in 1888. In the science of winemaking alone, "Pasteur's discoveries mark a crucial turning point in the history of wine."[12]

France's second major contribution to wine history arose in the château-designated vineyards of Bordeaux. By the nineteenth century, Bordeaux's wines had gained an aesthetic status as the benchmarks of wine quality, propelled by the popularity of the region's white Sauternes and especially its red clarets. The best wines produced came from a specific château, a term referring to a fortified citadel during the Middle Ages but morphing over time to mean a grape-growing estate and the wines it crafted. In 1855, Napoleon III, emperor of France, sought to showcase his country's wines in a universal exposition in Paris and invited Bordeaux's Chamber of Commerce to organize the exhibit. The chamber delegated the responsibility of ranking their region's chateau-designated wines to a joint committee of the city's merchants and wine brokers. The committee, known as the Syndicat des Courtiers, categorized twenty-six late-harvest white wines and fifty-eight red wines. It assigned the red wines to separate tiers: four premier crus, or first growths, at the top; twelve second growths; fourteen third growths; eleven fourth growths; and seventeen fifth growths. The committee made its report public, and later that year the French government exhibited the wines at the Paris World's Fair. In the exhibition's immediate aftermath, Bordeaux's wine production tripled. The 1855 Bordeaux classification system, "which helped make fledgling [château] traditions permanent," remains relatively intact in France to this very day.[13]

Just as the spotlight shone on French wine, a catastrophe loomed just around the corner. In the mid-1860s, probably beginning in the Rhône Valley, the aphid-like insect phylloxera started feeding on grapevine roots, ultimately killing the vines. Within a decade, phylloxera destroyed vineyards throughout France, the rest of Europe, South Africa, Australia, New Zealand, and California. Exasperated growers tried flooding vineyards, dousing vines with chemicals, and even irrigating their crops with white wine, but nothing seemed to work. By the century's end, experts finally arrived at a solution to the phylloxera conundrum: grafting European vines onto phylloxera-tolerant American rootstock, which rendered the insect powerless. Vineyards in France and throughout the world were uprooted and replanted. Although France's wine-producing regions never fully recovered from the phylloxera disaster, the country succeeded in restoring its iconic status by the early twentieth century. In yet another innovation to ensure wine quality, France developed a detailed system of regulations known as the Appellation d'Origine Contrôlée in the 1930s. The new regulatory standards designated specific places where vineyards could be planted and defined how those wines must be made. Thus, when André Tchelistcheff enrolled in the Institute of National Agronomy in 1933, France had once again become "the motherland of wine."[14]

André's studies at the Institute of National Agronomy included a course in viticulture taught by Pierre Viala, the chairman of the

Agricultural Academy of France. Viala had attained iconic status in the wine world for his research on rootstock resistivity against phylloxera. André regarded Viala and enologist Frederic Bioletti, from the University of California, as "two of the most important figures in the history of viticulture, who saved the world from phylloxera." The institute was also connected to a viticultural-enological research station just outside of Paris named after Viala. André worked at this experimental station, which provided oversight for all of northeastern France, a region that included Champagne and Burgundy. Despite André's later fame for producing some of California's best Cabernet Sauvignons, his constant quest to produce a great Pinot Noir no doubt stems from his Burgundian experience. "I have a Bourgogne palate," André once said. "It is always harder to find a fine Burgundy than it is a Bordeaux, but when you do, oh my, it is well worth it."[15] In addition to André's work at the institute and its experimental station, he took a course on fermentation science at the Pasteur Institute in Paris. To make ends meet, André worked in the laboratories of Nicolas, one of France's largest commercial wine retailers, and at the famous champagne house Moët et Chandon in Epernay, and he moonlighted as an Apache dancer in Paris.[16]

The Apache (pronounced ah-POSH or ah-poe-SHAY) Dance originated among male Parisian street gangs in the late nineteenth century. Known for their knife-wielding bravado as well as their violent behavior, these gang members became known as Apaches and were likened to "ferocious" American Indians by turn-of-the-century reporters. The Apache Dance featured an aggressive, acrobatic street fight between a man and a woman. Oftentimes the female dance partner prevailed in the theatrical struggle, suggesting that the dance's origins may represent an expression of women's empowerment rather than masculine violence against women. Performed early on in districts such as Montmartre, the dance was appropriated by Parisian elites by the eve of World War I. Wealthy Parisians held costume balls in which guests, disguised as hooligans, witnessed the aggressive male-female pirouette.

Prominent jazz clubs throughout Paris featured celebrity dancers, as Apache dancing became wildly popular during the interwar period. André became a part-time Apache dancer, an avocation requiring extraordinary dexterity and athleticism, to pay for his studies and to support his family. Four decades later, during one of the Tchelistcheff's noteworthy blini (Russian crepe) parties organized exclusively for the Hoffman family, André sported a bandana and dagger, leaped onto a table, and astonished his audience at the Hoffman Mountain Ranch winery in Paso Robles by performing a version of the Apache Dance.[17]

By the late 1930s, André moved on from Apache dancing to serve as an assistant research enologist at the Institute of National Agronomy, working under Paul Marsais. The director of viticulture, Marsais succeeded Pierre Viala following Viala's death in February 1936. André also held a training post at the Pasteur Institute, where he studied wine microbiology and biological pest control methodologies. In addition to these ventures, André studied horticulture and floriculture at the Trade Aboriculture School at the Château de Versailles. In these prestigious venues, Tchelistcheff learned the importance of sanitation and vineyard management, as well as specialized techniques such as controlled malolactic fermentation. After the primary fermentation of wine, in which yeasts convert grape sugar into alcohol, winemakers can induce the transformation of malic acid to lactic acid via malolactic fermentation. Rather than allowing the conversion of malic acid to lactic acid happen naturally, which can take months, winemakers can introduce specific bacteria into the new wine to make this transformation happen more quickly and in a much more controlled fashion. Malolactic fermentation can soften the wine, create greater balance, and provide microbial stability. André later introduced and perfected cutting-edge techniques such as controlled malolactic fermentation in the Napa Valley.[18]

Paul Marsais regarded the young Russian émigré as one of his star pupils and told Tchelistcheff that he would be much better in research than in industry because he believed that André possessed the "ability to penetrate to the problem."[19] Blessed with a keen intellect, exceptional training, and cosmopolitan seasoning, André looked beyond France for career advancement. "Foreigners were looked down upon" in France, André said, so he considered enological opportunities in South America and the Far East. André built connections with the United States as well, having met enologist Albert Winkler from the University of California in 1937, but at the time Tchelistcheff thought that California "was too foreign for me."[20] In the same year, André tasted his first California wines at an international exposition in Paris. One wine in particular—a 1934 Wente "Sauternes, Valle d'Oro" from Livermore Valley—impressed Tchelistcheff and astounded his French colleagues, who could not believe that California had produced such a wonderful wine. California came calling again in 1938, when two visitors from Napa Valley arrived in Paris looking for a new viticulturist-enologist.[21]

When enologist Leon Bonnet fell ill and needed to retire, Georges de Latour, the owner of Napa Valley's Beaulieu Vineyard, needed to find a suitable replacement. A de Latour family vacation in France during the summer of 1938 presented the perfect opportunity to solicit the advice of a wine expert. Accompanied by his son-in-law, the marquis de Pins (Henri Galcerand, who was married to de Latour's daughter, Hélène), de Latour visited Paris's Institute of National Agronomy and met with Paul Marsais. De Latour told Marsais that he needed someone with the expertise to solve several technical problems at Beaulieu. "We don't need a manager," de Latour said, "we need a research man and manager." De Latour fantasized that Marsais might put his own name forward but, if not, assumed Marsais would at least recommend a Frenchman. Surprisingly, Marsais hesitated to put forward a native candidate because he worried that a Frenchman might struggle to assimilate in a foreign country. "But I have a man of a cosmopolitan background," Marsais said, "and I think will be the man for you. He is of Russian origin and speaks fluent French."[22]

André made a strong impression on de Latour during their initial meeting. In addition to his cosmopolitan background and fluency in at least six languages, Tchelistcheff had recently published a paper on controlled malolactic fermentation, a technique completely unknown in California. To his credit, de Latour did not try to sugarcoat the job opening at Beaulieu. He told André about the various chemical and pathological problems in the California wine industry and discussed other challenges lying ahead. De Latour then offered Tchelistcheff the position on the spot. André stood perplexed. On the one hand, accepting this challenge would place Tchelistcheff closer to his in-laws. Catherine's parents, sister, and two brothers had moved to the United States in the 1920s, settling in New York and San Francisco. In addition, André's wife spoke English, having learned it in a Catholic school in Shanghai during her family's Russian exile. On the other hand, André spoke little English; knew next to nothing about the living standards in Rutherford, California (the site of Beaulieu Vineyard); and feared that he might be moving his family into the Wild West frontier. Nonetheless, as André said, "I just decided to take the challenge without too much enthusiasm." When André told his wife about the imminent move to California, she thought he was joking. Quickly realizing otherwise, Catherine began to cry.[23]

That evening de Latour attended a dinner at the American Embassy in Paris, where he met Frances Perkins, the U.S. secretary of labor. De Latour told Perkins about his plan to hire the Russian viticulturist-enologist to work at his California winery. Indignant, Perkins scolded de Latour for even thinking about hiring a foreigner with a depression still going on in America. Despite his initial setback, de Latour persisted. The following morning he returned to the embassy accompanied by Tchelistcheff to plead his case with the consul general; however, the consul told them that a work visa at the time was "impossible." Flustered but relentless, de Latour wired journalist Leon Adams, the chairman of the Wine Institute in San Francisco, urging him to lobby the Enology Department at the University of California for its support. Adams collected affidavits from UC faculty members and from the editor of *Wines & Vines* attesting to California's critical shortage of enologists.

BV's general manager Nino Fabbrini petitioned the state of California, claiming that no one in the United States of America matched Tchelistcheff's enological qualifications. In addition, de Latour elicited a letter of recommendation from Paul Marsais, who touted Tchelistcheff's *exceptional* qualities concerning punctuality, ardor to work, intelligence and originality, conscientiousness and judgment." As a last resort, de Latour also dispatched a telegram to his good friend Hiram Johnson, a Republican senator from California. "Hiram, goddammit, I have to solve this," de Latour wrote. "I need Tchelistcheff within the next month." Days later, Tchelistcheff received a telegram from Senator Johnson advising him to collect his newly approved work visa at the U.S. Embassy.[24]

Having successfully hired and properly credentialed his new wine man, de Latour departed for California. The marquis de Pins, along with his wife, Hélène, remained in France to coordinate the Tchelistcheffs' journey to America. "Mr. de Latour was very generous with my family," André said. "Everything was done first class." Following their train journey from Paris to Le Havre, the de Pins–Tchelistcheff party boarded the *Ile-de-France* ocean liner for a weeklong voyage to New York City. "Pancho" Villa, the manager of Beaulieu's distribution center in New York, greeted André upon the Russian émigré's arrival in America. At one time Villa sang tenor at La Scala in Milan, Italy, but he immigrated to the United States after losing his singing voice. De Latour instructed Villa to guide Tchelistcheff through the New York cellar and allow him to sample all of Beaulieu's wines. Tchelistcheff observed that most of the wines being distributed were sacramental wines, a product that had allowed Beaulieu to thrive during Prohibition. André also noted that the cellar temperature seemed shockingly warm by European standards. Nonetheless, he dutifully tasted from each barrel and took meticulous notes. The dessert wines impressed André more than the table wines, with one notable exception: Tchelistcheff identified a few very impressive barrels of Cabernet Sauvignon. The moment of that taste discovery, André later said, proved to be "the master key [of] my success."[25]

Soon after André's encounter with Pancho Villa, Tchelistcheff and his family embarked on another train journey, this time across an entire continent. André marveled at the vastness and the beauty of America. Upon his arrival in San Francisco in September 1938, André immediately phoned Georges de Latour, who arranged a lunch meeting with André and directed his wife, Fernande, to take care of Catherine Tchelistcheff. Despite André's limited grasp of English, he had no problem communicating with de Latour, who spoke French fluently. In fact, de Latour, a native of France but now a naturalized American citizen, habitually spoke French in his household and insisted that only French could be spoken at the de Latour dinner table. Regardless, within a year of living in the United States, Tchelistcheff learned enough English to present a lecture on the importance of cork selection to students at the University of California, Davis. André learned English by listening carefully and watching American films with his son, Dimitri, at the movie theatre in St. Helena, a small Napa Valley town four miles north of Rutherford. André also believed that his knowledge of other languages gave him an advantage in learning English. At Tchelistcheff's age (thirty-seven at the time), however, he found it impossible to eliminate his "very strong Franco-Russian accent."[26]

The day after André's lunch meeting with de Latour, a beautiful black Cadillac collected the Tchelistcheffs at de Latour's Sacramento Street office in San Francisco. André sat in the back with Georges and Fernande. A uniformed Portuguese chauffeur drove the party north out of the city, crossed the Golden Gate Bridge, passed the dairy farms in Marin County, and traveled past hundreds of acres of plum orchards in the Carneros region. By the time the de Latour delegation drove past the tiny settlement of Napa, André began to see a few vineyards. Tchelistcheff's extraordinary journey, which began in the forests of central Russia, continued on the battlefields of Crimea, detoured to eastern Europe, and landed temporarily in France, now continued in the Napa Valley. In the late 1930s, California had barely started to recover from Prohibition, whereas Europe, in André's words, "was technically, scientifically, so much ahead of California." André now found himself in a position to bridge these two worlds by bringing his knowledge and practical experience in enology and viticulture to the vineyards of California. As Tchelistcheff approached the tiny hamlet of Rutherford in de Latour's black Cadillac, the autumnal setting must have seemed magnificent. André later reflected, "Napa Valley was the most beautiful place I'd ever seen."[27]

CHAPTER 4

Beautiful Place

Everything was dramatically bad.

—ANDRÉ TCHELISTCHEFF

The indigenous Wappo called the valley Napa, or "Land of Plenty."
Seminomadic hunter-gatherers, the Wappo inhabited the Napa Valley
region for thousands of years before Mexican and American settlers
arrived and displaced them. For millennia the Wappo subsisted on
the valley's bounteous supplies of fish, fowl, game, berries, and acorns,
and lived in small, communal villages along the area's riverbanks. The
Wappo, whose name derives from the Spanish *guapo* (brave), resisted
the foreign incursions into their territory but eventually fell victim
to disease, alcohol, and genocidal violence. On February 27, 1850, for
example, two dozen white vigilantes from Sonoma invaded George
Yount's Rancho Caymus hell-bent for an Indian hunt. Yount had
received his land grant of nearly twelve thousand acres from the Mexican government in 1836, and his ranch stretched from what is now
his namesake, Yountville, northward to just south of present-day St.
Helena. Originally from North Carolina, Yount was the region's first
Euro-American permanent settler as well as the first person to plant
grapevines in the Napa Valley. He demonstrated genuine compassion
for the Wappo people living on his ranch, employing them as laborers
and training them to till soil and shear sheep, and the Wappo recip-
rocated by teaching Yount how to dye wool and smoke game and

fish. Understandably, the senseless vigilante assault in 1850 left Yount embittered and bewildered. The white invaders set fire to a Wappo village on Yount's property and, according to a Sonoma correspondent, "chased near one hundred Indians to the mountains." The riders then proceeded upriver to Rancho Carne Humana, an expanse of territory that stretched from Yount's northern boundary to Calistoga. When they arrived, according to court documents, the vigilantes shot Indians indiscriminately, burned their lodges, and destroyed their stores of grain. Yount, an eyewitness to the carnage, said the perpetrators "left [the Rancho] covered with the slain men, women, and children. . . . How many victims fell in this murderous forey [sic] has never been and never will be known."[1]

When George Yount ventured into the Napa Valley in the late 1830s, he brought Mission grapevine cuttings given to him by Mariano Guadalupe Vallejo, a Californio general and, at the time, a government official of the Mexican Republic. As the valley's first viticulturist, Yount planted vineyards and produced moderate quantities of wine until his death in 1865. His wines won a few prizes at state fair competitions, but the Mission grape, which Spanish missionaries introduced to California, generally yielded mediocre results. For this reason, nurserymen and viticulturists throughout the state searched for better grape varietals. Agoston Haraszthy, a Hungarian émigré who settled in California in 1849, became one of the most important leaders in this effort. Haraszthy believed in California's potential to produce wines on par with Europe's best, and eventually he imported over three hundred different grapevine cuttings from Europe. In 1856 Haraszthy purchased an acreage northeast of the town of Sonoma, land he described as "admirably adapted to the cultivation of the grape," and named it Buena Vista Farm. Rapidly Buena Vista became one of the most famous California wineries of its era. The restless, enterprising Hungarian American poured capital into his enterprise and constructed a luxurious Pompeiian-style villa overlooking his vineyards, by this time the most expansive in the United States. After a decade of growth, however, financial woes forced Haraszthy to sell his beloved Buena Vista. In 1868 the ambitious entrepreneur left California for Nicaragua, bought a plantation, and began distilling spirits from sugar cane. The following year Haraszthy disappeared forever while trying to cross a treacherous Nicaraguan river. His family speculated that he was either dragged underwater by alligators or swept out to sea.[2]

During his glory days at Buena Vista, Haraszthy employed a young German intellectual named Charles Krug, who had immigrated to the United States in 1847 and taught briefly in Philadelphia. When revolutionary turmoil erupted throughout Europe the following year, Krug had returned to his homeland to join fellow liberals in an unsuccessful effort to unify the fragmented German states. His progressive spirit undiminished, Krug then returned to America in 1852 and started a German-language newspaper in San Francisco that gave voice to his liberal viewpoints. Two years later, he purchased a farm south of San Francisco, met Agoston Haraszthy, and became a close associate of the flamboyant Hungarian. Krug accompanied Haraszthy to Sonoma in 1856 and worked as an apprentice winemaker at Buena Vista. In 1858 he borrowed Haraszthy's cider press, crossed the Mayacamas Mountains into Napa Valley, and made twelve hundred gallons of wine for the vineyardist John Patchett. Two years later, Krug moved to the Napa Valley permanently, settling just north of St. Helena. He married Caroline Bale, the daughter of English physician Edward Bale, the original owner of Rancho Carne Humana. Caroline's dowry included 540 acres of her father's property, and one year later Krug planted grapevines on it and built a winery. Krug became a major leader in local and statewide viticultural organizations and soon became recognized as Napa Valley's most prominent vintner. By the time of his death in 1892, which was memorialized by one of the most elaborate funerals in Napa Valley history, Krug's cellars held 800,000 gallons of wine.[3]

Following the lead of Agoston Haraszthy and fellow Napa Valley vintner George Belden Crane, who started his winery just south of St. Helena in 1859, Krug turned away from the inferior Mission grape and began planting imported grapevines by the late 1860s. The vines included Zinfandel, White Riesling, Palomino, Cinsaut, Grenache, Carignane, Mourvèdre, Charbono, and Bordeaux varietals such as Cabernet Sauvignon, Malbec, and Sémillon. The shift toward foreign vines marked a crucial turning point in Napa Valley wine history. Wine production in the valley increased tenfold between 1870 and 1880. By the end of the nineteenth century, Napa led California in gallons produced, surpassing Sonoma and Los Angeles Counties, the previous leaders. Krug's success in producing superior table wines using *vinifera* grape varietals attracted other opportunistic European adventurers to the "land of plenty." Most notable among them were two German siblings and a Finnish sea captain.

Between 1868 and 1888, over two million Germans immigrated to America, more than any other non-English-speaking nationality in that era. Two of the immigrants, brothers Jacob and Frederick Beringer, represented the handful of Germans who eventually made their way to Napa Valley. Originally from the Rhineland city of Mainz, where Jacob worked in winemaking and coopering, the Beringer brothers first settled in New York. Frederick started a malted barley business, and Jacob worked as a cellar foreman. In 1869 Jacob left for California, moved to Napa Valley, and was hired as Charles Krug's cellar master. In 1875 Jacob, with Frederick's backing, purchased a ninety-seven-acre ranch on the northwest side of St. Helena. Two years later Jacob employed Chinese laborers to excavate a winery cellar that became recognized as one the finest in the valley. From the 1860s to the 1880s, Chinese workers dug by hand many of Northern California's most impressive underground cellars and served as the principal labor force for virtually all vineyard activities. Despite being paid a fraction of what their Caucasian counterparts earned, a nationwide depression in the 1870s gave rise to racist agitation against Chinese workers. After Congress passed the Chinese Exclusion Act in 1882, most Chinese workers fled the wine country and never returned.[4]

Within two years, Jacob Beringer expanded his wine production from 40,000 to 100,000 gallons. In early 1878, Jacob also left his position at Krug's winery to concentrate on his own successful wine-making operation. Frederick joined him as the financier in 1884 and initiated construction on a seventeen-room mansion. Known as the Rhine House, the Beringer showpiece was designed to re-create the Beringer family home on the Rhine River. With Frederick's extensive business connections on the East Coast, the Beringers bypassed the powerful San Francisco merchants and sold their wines directly to eastern dealers. As a result, their wine production soared. By the 1890s, however, a future that seemed so bright for successful vintners such as the Beringer brothers collided with a new reality: a phylloxera epidemic ravaged Napa Valley's vineyards.[5]

Beginning in the 1870s, the phylloxera pestilence traveled slowly at first in the Napa Valley but became widespread by the 1890s. Even Inglenook, the region's most spectacular château winery, suffered from the pernicious infestation. Inglenook, which means "cozy chimney corner," was founded by George Yount's son-in-law William C. Watson as a small winery and sanatorium west of Rutherford. Between 1879 and 1881, Gustave Niebaum purchased the Inglenook property and some of its adjoining parcels, giving him a thousand-acre estate. A Finnish mariner by training, Niebaum made his fortune in the Alaska fur trade. During Niebaum's business travels associated with his San Francisco–based Alaska Commercial Company, he visited some of Europe's most spectacular châteaus. The winery visitations made a lasting impression. Niebaum assembled a prodigious library on winegrowing and, like Haraszthy, grew confident in California's potential to compete with the greatest wines of Europe. Following his purchase of Inglenook, Niebaum hired the engineer Hamden W. McIntyre to manage the estate and commissioned a San Francisco architect to construct a château as stylish as the wines he sought to produce. Niebaum's commitment to the highest standards of sanitation, combined with his utilization of the era's cutting-edge winemaking technologies, set Inglenook wines apart. He also employed estate bottling, a commercial practice unheard of in California at the time, that significantly enhanced quality control. With the addition of Niebaum's branding savvy, Inglenook's wines captured international awards and became marketable throughout the world. At its peak in the late nineteenth century, Inglenook produced eighty thousand gallons of premium wine. Despite its spectacular track record of success, Inglenook's production plummeted dramatically by the turn of the century, for as with so many other Napa Valley wineries, its vineyards fell victim to the phylloxera infestation.[6]

As the Europeans discovered, the solution to phylloxera required tearing out infected vines and replacing them with resistant ones. Given the considerable expense involved in this conversion, California vintners naturally felt compelled to plant grafted vines perfectly suited for the state's soils. As early as 1880, California's legislature recognized the growing economic importance of the state's wine industry. In that year, state legislators established the Board of State Viticultural Commissioners and appropriated funds to the College of Agriculture at the University of California, Berkeley. The legislature instructed both entities to undertake studies of the phylloxera and other vine pests and diseases, and to disseminate their findings to the viticultural industries. Over the next two decades, painstaking research took place, drawing upon some of the key insights of French enologist Pierre Viala (one of Tchelistcheff's mentors), and determined that the native species *Vitis rupestris,* or St. George rootstock, showed the most promise for California's vineyards. By the turn of the century, Napa Valley became the scene of frenzied replanting. During the 1901 planting season, 600,000 *vinifera* vines, grafted on rooted St. George cuttings, were sold in the St. Helena area alone. The following year, the forty-year-old enterprising businessman Georges de Latour placed an advertisement in the *St. Helena Star* offering St. George rootstock for sale.[7]

De Latour understood the gravity of the phylloxera crisis when it peaked in Napa Valley in the 1890s. As a youngster growing up in southwestern France, Georges watched his family's vineyards wither as a result of the root-sucking louse. Following the untimely deaths of the teenager's mother and father, friends of the family continued to raise de Latour and sent him to prestigious schools, including the École Centrale in Paris. De Latour studied the classics—in later years, Georges could still speak Greek and Latin, and quote verbatim from the *Odyssey* and *Julius Caesar*—and completed his degree in organic chemistry. In his late twenties, the intelligent, enterprising Frenchman left France for America, settled in the San Francisco Bay Area, and utilized his chemical knowledge to start a cream of tartar company based in San José. Cream of tartar is made from crystallized potassium bitartrate that forms on the inside of wine fermentation tanks. De Latour's workforce, and sometimes even himself, extracted the crusty sediment with chisels and hatchets, bagging it in hundred-pound sacks. By the end of the nineteenth century, de Latour's California Tartar Works extracted tartaric acid residues from virtually every large winery in Northern California. De Latour's deep familiarity with wine country at the time also convinced him that phylloxera would likely force every winery to uproot its infected vines and replant resistant ones.[8]

In 1898 de Latour married Fernande Romer, a young stenographer at his office headquarters in San José. Fernande was born in Alsace-Lorraine to German parents, grew up in the United States, and developed a de Latour–like business savvy. In later years, Tchelistcheff reminisced about Madame de Latour's intelligent management style. "She was a perfectionist who built the winery along with her husband," André said. The de Latours settled in the Sonoma town of Healdsburg, the site of one of his company's processing plants. In the late nineteenth century, Georges's business interactions put him in direct contact with all of the major wine producers in Sonoma and Napa Counties. During his carriage rides throughout the region, de Latour became particularly impressed with the climate and soils around Rutherford, located in the heart of Napa Valley. When he learned that a portion of Charles P. Thompson's Rutherford ranch was for sale, he took Fernande to see it. She fell in love with the site and began referring to it as *Beaulieu* (Beautiful Place). In 1900 the de Latours sold the Healdsburg business and purchased 4 acres of the Thompson property with the sale's proceeds. They retained their elegant home on Scott Street in San Francisco but now owned a beautiful country retreat as well. Owning property in the potential wheelhouse of quality wine production prompted the de Latours to launch a new business venture. In 1903 they purchased the remaining 128 acres of the Thompson property (calling it BV Ranch Number 1), began planting grapevines, and incorporated Beaulieu Vineyard the following year. During this same period, de Latour also established his own nursery near Paris, from which he imported *vinifera* vines grafted onto St. George rootstock. By the time of BV's incorporation in 1904, de Latour had become the leading seller of phylloxera-resistant vines in Napa Valley.[9]

As profits escalated from the sale of French-grafted wine imports as well as his other business ventures, Georges de Latour decided to produce his own wine. Up to this point, he had been buying wine in bulk from producers such as the Wente brothers in Livermore Valley (Alameda County), bottling it, and selling it to the Catholic Church. In fact, in 1904 de Latour's personal friendship with the archbishop of San Francisco earned BV the archdiocese's endorsement to serve as the church's sole supplier of sacramental wine. The shift from brokering wine to producing it represented a major undertaking, and de Latour needed someone who could manage it. In 1907 he hired Joseph (Joe) Ponti to serve as his superintendent of wine production and vineyard operations. Ponti, an Italian immigrant who had worked alongside his friend Benito Mussolini laying bricks only one year earlier, held his position at BV for the next forty-three years. Also needing to expand his acreage, the de Latours at first leased and then purchased outright Henry Harris's Rutherford property in 1910. De Latour called it BV Ranch Number 2. Over the next decade, BV's wine production expanded, but a number of other commercial wineries in the valley closed shop in anticipation of Prohibition. As wineries sold out, the de Latours bought up their winery equipment as well as more vineyard land at bargain prices. Its special dispensation from the church virtually handed Beaulieu Vineyard an exclusive franchise to produce altar wine for Catholic dioceses across America. Thus, in 1920, when the onset of Prohibition wiped out much of the rest of California's commercial wine industry, the de Latours were positioned instead for further expansion and significant profitability.[10]

Utilizing stationery that identified BV as "The House of Altar Wines," Beaulieu's bulk wine sales soared during the Prohibition era. Of considerable significance to their success, the de Latours also built a nationwide marketing network for BV wines. The network included their own Beaulieu Vineyard Distributing Company in New York and marketing arrangements with beverage distributors in Cleveland, Milwaukee, Omaha, Chicago, and Cincinnati. BV distributed wine in San Francisco and Los Angeles directly from the winery. Beaulieu shipped its wine in barrels to licensed wholesalers, who then resold it in smaller containers or bottles. BV's bulk wine sales of sacramental wine as well as sweet and "industrial" wines (used to flavor tobacco) remained its bread and butter even after Prohibition's repeal. BV did not distribute its estate-bottled wines nationally until 1937, when it contracted with the New York distributor Park & Tilford.[11]

In 1923 the de Latours purchased the first blocks of BV Ranch Number 3, a prune orchard located next to the Silverado Trail, from the Catholic Church. During the same year, they bought the old Seneca Ewer winery located in Rutherford across the road from BV Ranch Number 1. Designed by Inglenook's manager Hamden McIntyre in the mid-1880s, the spacious stone structure enabled BV to expand its production dramatically. At the same time, BV continued to ship wines provided by bonded suppliers, including the Wente brothers of Livermore Valley and the Sebastiani family in Sonoma. The Wentes, for example, delivered 30,000 gallons of Sémillon to BV each year between 1920 and 1933. The extraordinary volume of wine BV sold through the diocesan network—over 200,000 gallons in 1933 alone—likely "surpassed any ritual consumption by the most assiduous congregations."[12]

Nonetheless, as Ernest Wente pointed out, "when Prohibition ended [in 1933], BV was in the driver's seat."[13]

André later recalled one of Georges de Latour's typical business transactions from the late 1930s. He invited his friend and wine supplier Sam Sebastiani to a lunch at the Rutherford estate to discuss the possible purchase of an additional 250,000 gallons of sweet wine to fill out the BV inventory. Before the business negotiations even commenced, Sebastiani was treated to hors d'oeuvres, French champagne, and a three-hour multicourse meal, finished with a high-quality Algerian Armagnac and French coffee. Meanwhile, André's good friend August Sebastiani, Sam's son, waited outside patiently in his father Model T. Ford. Finally, Sam offered to sell his wine for eighteen cents a gallon. De Latour jumped out of his chair and exclaimed, "Why, Sam, are you going to put me in the poorhouse? I am broke. I am broke." After two more hours of futile back-and-forth bargaining, Sebastiani politely kissed the hand of Madame de Latour and stood up to leave. "Sam, my friend, you are not going to do such a thing to me," Georges said. "Let's have another cigar." Two hours later, the men finally settled on a price of fifteen and a half cents for Muscat and twelve and a half cents for Angelica. "Georges de Latour had a sense of humor and a way of making his deals in his own classical European traditional way," André said. Tchelistcheff regarded de Latour's approach as an effective and "very rational way of doing business."[14]

Up to this point, de Latour's savvy negotiating skills and sound business decisions paid off handsomely. After all, Beaulieu's essential purpose was to generate income for the de Latour family. Yet Georges also aspired for winemaking excellence. He wanted BV to be known as more than the nation's leading supplier of altar wines. Specifically, de Latour wanted BV to rival France, the standard-bearer of quality wine, in the production of a world-class Bordeaux-style claret. For this reason, he traveled to his homeland in the late 1930s, landed Paul Marsais's handpicked wine man, and delivered him to California. When André Tchelistcheff emerged from his employers' black Cadillac in the tiny hamlet of Rutherford in September 1938, he could hardly believe his eyes. André described the de Latour estate as an "unbelievable paradise" with its lush gardens, uniformed servants, and magnificent Spanish-style mansion with eleven bedrooms and bathrooms. Overawed, Tchelistcheff later explained his first reaction: "After all, please remember that I was just a Russian immigrant, and I lived with a very tight belt all my life since I left home." The grandeur, the beauty, and the expense seemed unbelievable. "Everything was just classical," André said.[15]

The de Latours prepared a luncheon feast for the awestruck Russian exile that included crawfish, trout, pheasant, and BV's best wines. As was customary, Georges dressed in black tie, and Madame de Latour donned an elegant hat for the dining occasion. A butler seated the guests, and uniformed maids served the meal. For the broiled trout, freshly caught from an artificial stream on the property, Georges opened a bottle of Sémillon (labeled "Sauternes") produced by the Wente brothers. The greatness of the white wine shocked André. "It was really, honestly comparable with the great, great châteaux Sauternes in France," André said. With the pheasant, also raised on the estate, de Latour opened a 1919 Cabernet Sauvignon as well as an award-winning 1918 "Burgundy," which blended Cabernet with Pinot Noir. Unlike the Sémillon, BV's reds were produced by de Latour himself while working with his winemaker-superintendent, Joseph Ponti. In effect, de Latour had served as BV's first enologist before hiring Leon Bonnet, who preceded Tchelistcheff and had studied under the great enologist Frederic Bioletti. The food, the wine, and the heritage of Beaulieu no doubt impressed André on that September day. So far, all of the vibes registered positively for de Latour's new enologist.[16]

Following breakfast the next morning, Ponti collected André in a Model T Ford pickup and gave him a tour of the BV vineyards. Tchelistcheff wore a necktie and white laboratory jacket, which he described as a "compulsory necessity." André first took note of the Cabernet vine spacings, which were triple or even quadruple the volume of Bordeaux.

The spacing as well as the entire method of cultivation seemed "absolutely foreign" to Tchelistcheff. Following a survey of the vineyards, Ponti drove him to the loading platform, where he was introduced to BV's employees and taken on a tour of the winemaking facilities. The "primitiveness" of the entire operation shocked Tchelistcheff. "I was amazed to see . . . such an obsolete system of winemaking, without any sign of scientific-industrial interpretation," André said. He found the lack of controlled sanitation and general filth throughout the winery appalling. André even witnessed a rat swimming in a tank of white wine. Imagine what Pasteur would think? The shocking revelation, coming on the heels of such positive impressions from the day before, must have mortified Tchelistcheff. As he later observed, "Everything was dramatically bad."[17]

Over the next three weeks, Tchelistcheff conducted microbiological and chemical analyses of BV's complete wine inventory. He discovered that over half of the table wines stored at BV were infected with *Acetobacter*, with a volatile acidity approaching vinegar status. André reported his discovery to de Latour, who prompted BV to liquidate nearly 300,000 gallons of its damaged wine to large distilling houses. Tchelistcheff then focused his attention on remedying BV's sanitation failures. First, he instructed his winery workers to sterilize the fermentation tanks with the oxidizer potassium permanganate. Next, André ordered the replacement of the must lines, which were clogged with iron oxide (rust). The antiquated equipment at BV included cast-iron crushers and pumps, as well as brass couplings. As a result, wines came to the fermentation tanks with a high concentration of heavy metals, further adulterating their quality. "The process of crushing, of primary fermentation was conducted in a very unbelievable, primitive way," André said. In addition to using inferior equipment, BV initially had no reliable means of temperature control. To lower the temperature during fermentation, workers dumped blocks of ice into the tanks, effectively diluting the wine. All of these deficiencies resulted in carloads of damaged wine being sent back to BV to be dumped. When André came to California, he expected to find a "progressive, technological empire." Instead, he discovered a wine industry "absolutely, negatively . . . blind." By Tchelistcheff's reckoning, California lagged a half century behind France in vinification and temperature-control technologies.[18]

Other quality-control issues bothered Tchelistcheff "tremendously." For example, when André first arrived in Napa Valley, winemakers routinely doused their vineyards with sacks full of sulfur (potassium metabisulfite) and used bucketloads of the compound during fermentation. Used in moderation, sulfur neutralizes unwanted bacteria. André "normalized" the application of sulfur at BV by diluting it during fermentation and introducing sulfuring machines in the vineyards that began sulfuring the vines at a rate of ten pounds per acre rather than one pound per vine! Tchelistcheff also objected to what he considered the "liberal interpretation of the law of ecology" in Napa Valley. When he arrived in California, he encountered vineyards planted with varietals from Burgundy, Bordeaux, Spain, Portugal, Moselle, and the Rhine. The pioneers who came to Napa Valley thought they had found paradise on earth, André reasoned, so they had felt entitled to plant what they pleased. In 1938 BV itself produced a line of over thirty different varietals regardless of their suitability for the Rutherford appellation. As the product of European agricultural science, Tchelistcheff recognized the centrality of soil and climate in viticulture to the ecology provided by Mother Nature rather than what he called "managerial ecology." André considered himself "a great believer that everything in winemaking, in the wine industry and wine philosophy and morals, is directly connected with ecology."[19]

On top of all these technical failures and philosophical blunders, Tchelistcheff encountered a culture of secrecy that pervaded Napa Valley in the late 1930s. When André first arrived at BV, Joe Ponti told him that sharing any technological secrets with BV's neighboring wineries was strictly prohibited. For example, when BV introduced refrigeration to better control fermentation, Ponti placed the Frigidaire compressors above the tanks where no one could see them. Ponti, a pragmatic, self-made winemaker, argued repeatedly with Tchelistcheff over the next two decades. He regarded André as an arrogant prima donna. "After all, I was the winemaker," Ponti said. "If [Tchelistcheff] was going to interfere, I would tell him to get away from me." André later admitted that his perfectionist tendencies made him "very abrasive" to some people. "But to achieve a goal, sometimes you must insist on having your way," he said. Even Warren Winiarski later pointed out that André could "be imperious, abrupt, impatient with sloppy procedures." Nonetheless, Tchelistcheff was also "poetic, visionary, romantic." André possessed two geniuses, according to Winiarski: "dry-eyed, rigorous exactitude, and generous leaps of imagination— non-rigid, non-uniform, and innovative."[20]

André later downplayed his acrimonious relationship with Ponti, yet he still regarded the Italian immigrant's secretive approach as incomprehensible. André recognized that de Latour had traveled all the way to France to hire someone who could help reform an industrial culture gutted by Prohibition and rebuild Napa Valley's reputation in its wake, but Tchelistcheff never imagined the challenges he now faced. He experienced sixteen-hour workdays and sleepless nights worrying about the various difficulties. To make matters worse, tensions mounted at home. For example, on Dimitri's first day of school in Rutherford, Catherine sent her son to the one-room schoolhouse dressed in the short pants that schoolchildren in France customarily wore. Dimitri's classmates mocked his appearance, pelted him with oranges, and delivered a sound beating that sent him home in tears. André tried his best to comfort Dimitri as well as his wife, who struggled for years in her own adjustment to rural California. As these painful experiences accumulated, Tchelistcheff began to contemplate leaving BV after the first harvest. After all, "I *never* thought that I was going to America to stay," André later observed.[21]

Why then did Tchelistcheff decide to stay? As André once pointed out, "Anything that happens to me in my life, it just happens by necessity." Therefore, one essential reason keeping André in California rather than returning to Europe must certainly have been the political uncertainties associated with Nazi expansionism. Nazi Germany's occupation of Czechoslovakia in March 1939 followed by its invasion of Poland in September destabilized eastern Europe and provoked the Second World War. The capitulation of France to the Germans the following May dashed any hope of returning to western Europe as well. Another reason André stayed in Rutherford was due to Georges de Latour's confidence in Tchelistcheff's expertise and for virtually granting him a "carte blanche in the re-modernization of Beaulieu." The quality of many California wines, reputed to be suitable only for winos by the late 1930s, had fallen dramatically as a result of Prohibition. To rebuild California's reputation for producing high-quality wines, "there was a necessity to really put something new into the industry," André said. "So that is why they selected me to proceed with all these reforms." Tchelistcheff began his process of reform with important controlled sanitation measures, but he also harbored long-range goals for improving wine quality by capitalizing on his background in fermentation science and viticulture. Most important, he sought to apply Europe's ecological or "appellation of origin" approach to California winemaking by matching the finest grape varietals to their appropriate soil and microclimate. André felt a professional, even spiritual obligation to bridge the gap between grape growing and winemaking by merging viticulture and enology.[22]

Georges de Latour's small lots of Cabernet Sauvignon provided another compelling reason for Tchelistcheff to stay. Soon after André arrived at BV, de Latour invited him to sample from a barrel of his 1936 vintage Cabernet. The wine impressed André, who possessed an exceptional palate despite being a habitual smoker (even into his late eighties). The wine displayed brilliant aromas and flavors, a velvety mouthfeel, and a long finish. Tchelistcheff also detected the expression of Rutherford's distinct terroir, which he later referred to as "Rutherford Dust." Pleased by Tchelistcheff's positive response, de Latour told André that the 1936 Cabernet surpassed any wine BV ever made.

"Moreover," de Latour said, "it shows what is possible. I want all of my wines to be that good. That's why I have brought you here." The following year the 1936 BV Cabernet Sauvignon won a gold medal at the 1939 Golden Gate International Exposition in San Francisco. Georges never lived to see the release of what came to be called the Georges de Latour Private Reserve Cabernet Sauvignon, California's first cult Cabernet. Diagnosed with cancer in 1939, de Latour died the following February at the age of eighty-three. Later that year, BV released the wine that made it famous. De Latour, Ponti, and Bonnet made the 1936 Cabernet, although Tchelistcheff guided it through the classical European method of aging, using the small cooperage of French and American origin. With the release of this vintage, people began to take note of André's work. "I managed to become, let's say, a prophet . . . a prophet of Napa Valley in Cabernet styling," André said.[23]

Fernande de Latour, who already played a central role in Beaulieu's business decisions, replaced her late husband as president of BV and supervised the winery until her death in 1951. André regarded Madame de Latour as a "perfectionist" who took a more "aggressive" approach to business decisions than her husband did. For example, when the ninety-acre Martin Stelling Jr. property in Rutherford became available in 1943, she jumped at the opportunity, making it BV Ranch Number 4. Tchelistcheff also admired Madame's grace and intelligence, in keeping with his affection for the entire de Latour family. Dagmar Sullivan, Fernande's granddaughter, always regarded André as her surrogate father and often sought his wise counsel when feeling troubled. Dagmar's son, Walter III, referred to Tchelistcheff as "Uncle André." "I felt very close to him, and he in turn was very close to our family," Sullivan said. Walter added that André "was a wonderful storyteller [and] would tell us about when he was a youngster in the summertime he would go fishing with his family in Siberia, and just tell us that it was an absolute oasis when it came to outdoor activities and being a sportsman." In his later years, André recalled his many conversations with the de Latour family. "I miss them very much," André said.[24]

It took André two years to replace the must lines, coating their interior with expensive Pyrex glass to avoid introducing heavy metals into the wine. He also addressed BV's flawed bottling procedures, which introduced oxygen into the wines throughout each stage of the process. In addition, Tchelistcheff built a cold room for fermenting white wine. He understood the importance of temperature-controlled fermentation in producing crisp, dry whites comparable to French Chablis. André also continued to work tirelessly in what he called his "little tiny" laboratory at Beaulieu, experimenting with new enological techniques. During the late 1930s and early 1940s, a new generation of wine people, hungry for knowledge, came to the valley. Tchelistcheff began to mentor them. In 1939 André hired his first assistant, Eugene Seghesio, a recent graduate of the University of California. Seghesio, whose immigrant parents, Edoardo and Angela, had established a successful winery in Sonoma County in 1902, derived his zeal for wine-making from his Italian heritage. Bard Suverkrop, another Berkeley graduate, came next and started working with André on malolactic fermentation. In the early 1940s, they coauthored a paper titled "The Approach to Malo-lactic Fermentation in California Red Wines" and presented it to the American Chemical Society in San Francisco.[25]

By the 1940s, BV ranked among the "big four" producers of quality table wines among the approximately sixty-five wineries in the Napa Valley, providing further evidence of Georges and Fernande de Latours' business acumen and Tchelistcheff's technical skill. Inglenook, Beringer, and Larkmead Winery rounded out the list. Unlike BV, Inglenook rarely sold wine in bulk, focusing its entire production on estate-bottled table wines. André regarded Inglenook as the number 1 château of Napa Valley at the time because of its approach, and he greatly admired Inglenook's owner, John Daniel Jr. Gustave Niebaum's grandnephew took ownership of the winery upon the death of Gustave's widow in 1936. Beringer favored a business model similar to BV's, bottling some of its wine under its own label but selling most of it in bulk to be blended and bottled elsewhere. The Larkmead Winery was located three miles north of Beringer on the valley floor. The Salmina family, originally from Switzerland, purchased the property in 1892. Eking out an existence during Prohibition, Larkmead positioned itself after the repeal to offer, in its words, "the very choicest aged wines made exclusively from Napa Valley grapes." In 1937 two of Larkmead's varietal wines, a Cabernet and Zinfandel, took first prizes at the California State Fair. That same year, Larkmead, Beringer, and Inglenook received a *diplôme d'honneur* from the Paris International Exposition.[26]

Under Tchelistcheff's guidance, BV's best wines became wines of distinction beginning in the 1940s; they were served at White House dinners and poured for traveling European dignitaries. BV wines appeared on restaurant lists at some of the most exclusive hotels in the world, including New York's Waldorf Astoria, Boston's Ritz-Carlton, and the Hotel George V in Paris. Beaulieu's wines also flowed at banquets honoring notable guests such as Winston Churchill, Dwight Eisenhower, Douglas MacArthur, Anthony Eden, and Charles de Gaulle. The influence and impact of BV's Private Reserve in particular was directly attributable to Tchelistcheff's winemaking skill. André insisted on twenty-four months of bottle aging, proper clonal grape selection, small cooperage, control of malolactic fermentation, and egg-white fining. He approached each task with ironclad determination and legendary stamina. During the harvest and crush, André used to sleep near the vats in the winery. As André characterized it, "When my wines utter enological sounds, I want to be there to hear them and make the necessary wine adjustments." Equally important, he recognized the significance of managing the grapevines and spent more time in the vineyards than in the winery itself. He once said, "When I am tired, exhaustedly tired . . . I used to go in the evenings alone in the vineyards and just relax by talking to [the vines]." Based on his successes in the 1940s, Tchelistcheff even ventured temporarily into winery ownership. He partnered with newspaper magnate Frank Bartholomew to purchase Buena Vista Winery in Sonoma, investing $2,000 in the venture. Shortly thereafter, however, André sold his interest in the winery to Bartholomew but remained as Frank's consultant. It proved to be André's first and last attempt to own a winery.[27]

Despite BV's rapid ascent in the wine world in the 1940s, it experienced a major setback in the summer of 1947 when a fire, which started in the winery's roof insulation, destroyed approximately 600,000 gallons of wine. Why the roof caught fire was never satisfactorily determined, but possibly it resulted from a workman's discarded cigarette. André watched helplessly as the fire completely destroyed the fermenting room and cooperage cellar. Rutherford's fire chief at the time, Louis Tonella, reported that his firefighters "stayed outside and squirted water" but essentially "let it burn." It took until midnight to contain the fire, and when Tonella's crew opened the backdoor, "a flood of wine about three feet deep came out" and flowed into the Napa River. Fortunately for Beaulieu, the stone section of the original Seneca Ewer winery escaped damage, preserving the entire stock of the '47 Georges de Latour Private Reserve Cabernet. Along with the 1946 BV Pinot Noir, which André always regarded as his greatest wine, the '47 Private Reserve ranked among the best of his Cabernets.[28]

Prior to BV's catastrophic fire, in Tchelistcheff's recollection, he launched an initiative that more than made up for Beaulieu's temporary setback. With Madame de Latour's blessing, André opened the Napa Valley Enological Research Center in St. Helena. One impetus for this endeavor was the powerful Bank of America, which held a financial stranglehold over virtually every winery in Napa Valley except Beaulieu and required each mortgaged winery to provide monthly certificates of sanitation from a certifiable source. The regulation incentivized Tchelistcheff to open a facility where he could conduct research as a paid consultant. As André put it, the Bank of America's control "was the bread of my laboratory." Another factor influencing his initiative was the shortage of academic expertise available at UC-Davis's fledgling Enology Department. Only one enologist, Dr. Albert Winkler, escaped the draft during the Second World War. Finally, Tchelistcheff felt duty bound to continue expanding his own winemaking knowledge and to share it with others. Specifically, he envisioned significant advantages in building a network of winemakers who could all benefit from mutual collaboration. As André fully understood, Napa Valley's secretive wine culture severely hampered any future progress for the region. "In those days everything was surrounded by secrecy," André later reflected. "There was no communication allowed between winemakers—no friendship among winemakers." These circumstances needed to change, prompting André to invent a new strategy for bridging the divide. Among all of his contributions to the rebirth of the Napa Valley wine industry, his St. Helena research lab ranks near the top. It attracted some of that era's most visionary wine people, including John Daniel of Inglenook, Louis P. Martini, August Sebastiani, Lee Stewart of Souverain, and two up-and-coming brothers from the Charles Krug Winery, Robert (Bob) and Peter Mondavi.[29]

20 Septembre 1938. Paris.

Au Laboratoire de Viticulture Pierre Viala
de l'Institut national agronomique

1. André (*far right*) with colleagues at Paris's Institute of National Agronomy
on September 28, 1938. Courtesy of Dorothy Tchelistcheff.

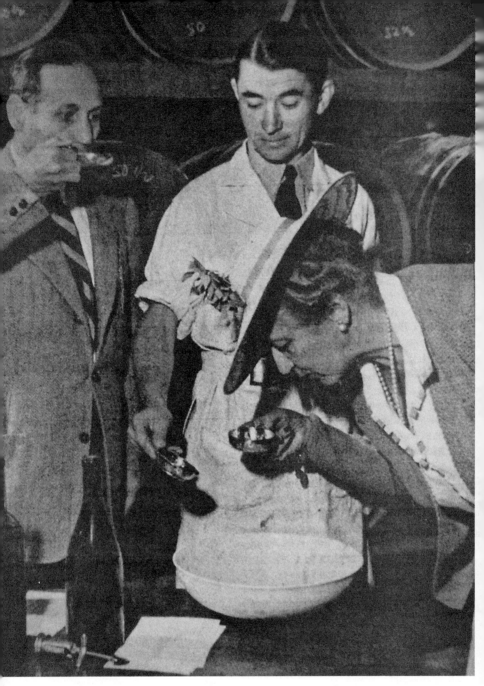

2. André providing wine samples to Fernande de Latour and her son-in-law, Galcerand de Pins, in 1942. Courtesy of Dorothy Tchelistcheff.

3. Second floor of the Richie Building in St. Helena, where André established his enological laboratory shortly after World War II. Photograph by author.

4. André in 1967. Courtesy of Dorothy Tchelistcheff.

5. André inside a barrel room. Courtesy of Dorothy Tchelistcheff.

CHAPTER 5

The Mentor

I am very proud that in several of these men I was able
to create this deep interest . . . of living in wine and
trying to concentrate all of [one's] life to the wine.

—ANDRÉ TCHELISTCHEFF

Among the scores of future winemakers André mentored over the
years, he regarded Bob Mondavi as one of his best students. Mondavi's
parents, Cesare and Rosa, grew up near the small town of Sassoferrato
in central Italy. They immigrated to America in the early twentieth
century, settling first in Minnesota and then journeying west to Lodi,
California, in 1923. The couple raised four children—two daughters
and two sons. Bob, the elder son, was born in 1913, and his brother,
Peter, followed fourteen months later. Cesare established a successful
grape and fruit wholesale business in Lodi, where the Mondavi family
became prominent members of the Italian American community. The
Mondavis generally thrived during Prohibition by shipping grapes
from California to family winemakers back east. Cesare and Rosa,
whose background included little formal schooling, nonetheless placed
a high value on education, at least for their sons. As a result, they sent
both Robert and Peter to Stanford, one of the West's most prestigious
universities. For Bob, in particular, the experience at Stanford was
transformative. As he later reflected, Stanford's professors taught him

to overcome his feelings of inadequacy, to open his mind and his heart, and to "use [his] own damn head!"[1]

Mondavi majored in economics and business at Stanford, but in his senior year, he took a chemistry course that piqued his interest in winemaking. As a result, he signed up for a summer crash course in viticulture and enology at the University of California, Berkeley, after his graduation in 1936. Later that summer Bob traveled to St. Helena and began working with Jack Riorda, one of his father's friends who owned a bulk wine business in the community. Soon thereafter Cesare purchased an interest in Riorda's business, which soon became known as Sunny St. Helena. Mondavi loved living in the valley, as it was home to a number of Italian immigrant families and an ideal setting for producing high-quality table wines. Meanwhile, Bob's brother, Peter, graduated from Stanford in 1937 and enrolled in a graduate program in enology at the University of California, Berkeley. Following graduation, Peter worked at a distillery in the Central Valley before enlisting in the U.S. Army Air Corps at the outset of World War II. Robert remained at Sunny St. Helena until 1943, having taken over as its manager when Riorda died three years earlier, and enjoyed considerable economic success. When the old Charles Krug property north of St. Helena came up for sale in 1943, the budding entrepreneur regarded it as the opportunity of lifetime in the winery business. Cesare reluctantly agreed to purchase the Krug ranch, which sold for $75,000, on one condition: his sons must always work together to build the business.[2]

Robert took over as the manager of the historic Krug property in 1943, while Peter was still serving abroad in the army. Without Peter's more advanced winemaking expertise, Mondavi needed help in getting started. With some trepidation, he reached out to the storied enologist at BV, André Tchelistcheff. "So I went [to see André] with my hat in my hand ... and said that I was very much interested in wanting to learn about the wine business," Mondavi said. With Madame de Latour's approval, André picked up his first paid consultancy at the

Krug Winery and held it over the next several years. He started meeting with Mondavi on a regular weekly basis after working hours to offer advice and share ideas. Mondavi later said that André "was willing to do everything." In fact, Robert speculated, "[André] built his lab when he found he was making enough money with me."[3]

Tchelistcheff's Enological Research Laboratory occupied the second floor of the Richie Building, the oldest structure on Main Street in St. Helena. It quickly became a magnet for area winemakers, especially a new breed of individuals eager to learn and anxious to transform the region's reputation. In addition to Robert Mondavi and his brother, Peter, they included John Daniel Jr. of Inglenook, Louis P. Martini, August Sebastiani, and Lee Stewart of Souverain. André and his colleagues gradually gelled into a brotherhood of wine professionals, calling it the Napa Valley Wine Technical Group. According to Martini, the loosely structured consortium started meeting on a regular basis to gab with one another and exchange technical information. For several years in the late 1940s, each member researched a particular subject and reported back to the entire group. Gradually the group organized more formal dinners, inviting guest lecturers from UC-Davis to attend. The group's collaborative spirit, a direct result of Tchelistcheff's research initiatives, provided the foundation for a cultural shift that defined valley winemaking for the next three decades. "There was a mutual effort by this group to achieve maximum quality," André said. "We all worked in research and we all worked together. These were dynamic men—all of them."[4]

André's close working relationship with the Charles Krug Winery paid off significantly for BV in 1947. In the aftermath of Beaulieu's catastrophic fire that year, Bob and Peter Mondavi accepted production of BV's white wines for the next two vintages. When Peter returned from the war, he joined the family winery and brought his considerable technical skills to the Krug operation. In particular, Peter's previous training at Berkeley exposed him to the latest research on the cold fermentation of white table wines. When Peter joined the Napa Valley

Wine Technical Group, he discovered a kindred spirit in Tchelist-cheff, who recognized the importance of cold fermentation based on his European training. For the Mondavis, the results were stunning. Between 1947 and 1956, the Mondavi brothers won more than a hundred California State Fair medals for their white table wines, more than any other California winery. Their success, attributable in part to their winemaking skills, also resulted from a willingness to invest in the latest refrigeration technology for white wine production. After BV contracted with Krug to produce its white wines in '47 and '48, André shepherded the entire de Latour family to the Krug Winery to show them its superior production facilities. The visible disparity between BV's and Krug's equipment convinced Madame de Latour to invest in a similar upgrade. André's strategic maneuver paid off.[5]

For a short period in the late 1940s, Tchelistcheff's successful Enological Research Laboratory in St. Helena enabled him to become, in his words, "completely independent" of Beaulieu Vineyard. At the time, "very few people knew that," André said. According to him, BV kept him on as its chief consulting contractor while he also consulted for Charles Krug, Martini, Inglenook, Sebastiani, and other wineries in Napa and Sonoma. During this time, André trained his son in his St. Helena laboratory, preparing Dimitri for a successful career first as a student at UC-Davis and then as a first-rate enologist in his own right. André later referred to his independent work in St. Helena as among "the most exciting years of my career." Bob Mondavi, André's close associate, recalled that Tchelistcheff was off BV's payroll briefly, but a recession at the end of the decade, giving rise to winery foreclosures and the loss of clients, forced André to return to Beaulieu. According to Mondavi, BV also realized how much André meant to its successful operation so "they hired him back."[6]

André's return coincided with another major transition at Beaulieu: on the twelfth of October 1951, Madame de Latour died at the age of seventy-five. During the course of a half century, Fernande and her husband, Georges, had succeeded in building one of the most celebrated wineries in America. Leadership at BV now passed to their daughter, Hélène, also known as the marquise de Pins. Her husband, Henri Galcerand de Pins or the marquis de Pins, owned the Château de Montbrun near Toulouse, France. The de Pins raised two children, a daughter named Dagmar and a son, Richard. Right after the war, Dagmar married Walter Sullivan, a Stanford graduate and successful San Francisco commercial real estate developer. Each year the de Pins split their time among three residences: their "country" house in Rutherford, an apartment in San Francisco, and the château in Montbrun. At each location, Hélène displayed her legendary hospitality, hosting social events and entertaining celebrities. For example, the de Pins's expensive Nob Hill apartment in San Francisco provided a setting for some of the most exclusive Bay Area cocktail parties in the postwar era. At the Beaulieu estate, Hélène entertained scores of luminaries over the years, including ambassadors from France, Denmark, and Great Britain, and The Who's lead guitarist, Pete Townshend. Guests ate scrumptious meals prepared by her French-speaking Japanese chef Roy Hiroaka and drank legendary wines from BV's cellar. The setting was also meant to impress: the beautiful white frame home was filled with expensive French antiques, was surrounded by ancient oak trees, had a tennis court and a swimming pool, and featured magnificent French and Italian gardens maintained by six full-time gardeners. Embracing the good life, the marquise de Pins cherished her royal status and behaved in accordance with her titled position. As far as she was concerned, the BV winery existed exclusively to sustain her royal lifestyle. Furthermore, its business model worked wonderfully well for a half century, so why make major changes to it? For the duration of her presidency at BV (1951–69), Hélène invested in upgrades to the winery with considerable reluctance and only for a fraction of its required needs. She told André that his job was "to keep operating the winery so it can keep money flowing to me according to my needs. I will not put any more money into that winery; that winery has the job of providing money for me. My father gave me his solemn promise."[7]

André adored Madame de Pins but argued with her incessantly over the technical deficiencies at BV. She tested his patience on more than one occasion, yet André put up with her eccentricities as few others could. In fact, his devotion to Hélène and her family never wavered. According to Madame's grandson Walter Sullivan III, André "was the *only* person [who] kissed my grandmother in her coffin" at her funeral in November 1982. Nevertheless, André did not understand how the marquise, so meticulous and detail oriented, could demand perfection in everything except her own winery. For example, workers once accidentally dumped soda ash that killed two shrubs planted alongside BV's champagne warehouse. Madame went ballistic when she learned about the mishap and phoned André to voice her complaint. André then approached Dick Peterson, his newly hired associate at Beaulieu. "Madame de Pins wants you to *personally* drop everything and go down to the nursery and buy two of those bushes and get them up here and get them planted immediately," André said. He then added, "It's too goddam bad it wasn't five acres of Pinot Noir. She wouldn't have cared about that." When Peterson first arrived at BV, André warned him that any winery repairs took a backseat to Madame de Pins's immediate needs. "Sometimes, my dear sir," André advised, "when you are repairing something in the winery with (maintenance manager) Bill Amaral, if Madame wants Bill to change a light bulb in her house or fix a door lock, you [must] drop everything and send Bill up to her house. Bill can do the winery job later."[8]

In addition to Beaulieu's leadership transition in 1951, the year featured an outstanding private reserve vintage as well as another soon-to-be famous André protégé named Joseph Heitz. Born in 1919, Heitz grew up in rural Illinois and briefly attended the University of Illinois at Urbana-Champaign. He majored in animal science with aspirations of becoming a veterinarian, but a lack of funds forced him to drop out. Following a brief stint with the flying cadets in Muskogee, Oklahoma, Heitz hitchhiked to California and landed a job at Northrop Aircraft Corporation in Hawthorne. Drafted at the outset of World War II, he spent the rest of the war stateside in Fresno, California. He served as a ground crew chief on Northrop's P-61 Black Widow, the first purposely built night-fighter aircraft. During his service in Fresno, Heitz also worked evenings at the Italian Swiss Colony winery and, after his discharge, decided to enroll in the enology program at the University of California, Davis. Heitz graduated in 1948; worked for a short period at E. & J. Gallo in its quality-control lab in Modesto, California; and then joined the Wine Growers Guild in Lodi. During his time at the guild, Heitz learned that Tchelistcheff's assistant Bard Suverkrop was leaving, opening up a coveted position at BV. "There was a certain amount of honor in the wine business," Heitz later said, and he knew that André could not hire him away from the guild, one of Tchelistcheff's paid consultancies. Therefore, Heitz took a calculated risk. He left the guild; signed on with the Mission Bell Winery in Madera, California; and prayed that Beaulieu would come calling. "[My wife Alice and I had] never fully unpacked at Mission Bell," Heitz said, when André phoned to offer Joe an assistant winemaker position at BV. Thrilled to be working alongside a master winemaker at one of the best wineries in America, Heitz felt that he "had arrived."[9]

Heitz worked at Beaulieu Vineyard between 1951 and 1958. His duties focused on quality control but extended beyond laboratory analysis. He also oversaw winery operations, monitoring barrel-washing standards and ensuring that the pumping was done correctly. Each morning Heitz arrived at the winery early to personally check each tank for temperature and sugar levels. At times Joe even went into the vineyards with André, learning a great deal about the subject. On Saturday mornings, Heitz accompanied André on trips to Sonoma to meet with Tchelistcheff's clients, always stopping at Buena Vista and Sebastiani. One of Heitz's first disagreements with André occurred over the final clarification, or "fining," of the '51 Private Reserve Cabernet Sauvignon. André insisted on using egg whites, whereas Joe preferred gelatin, which is much easier to use and somewhat cheaper. "I think that was the only disagreement that André and I had in the philosophy of winemaking," Heitz recalled. "So we finally settled it: half his way and half my way." Although BV bottled each version of the '51 separately, neither André nor Joe could tell the difference upon its release. Heitz also remembered that for André, every task in wine production merited "A-1 priority." He meant that "you don't have any second-rate jobs in a winery. You pay top attention to *everything*," Heitz recalled. "I learned a hell of a lot from André. I soaked it up from him for over eight years. He was a great addition to my life as a winemaker."[10]

Heitz left BV in 1958 to pioneer an enology program at Fresno State University. For three and a half years, Joe worked tirelessly to build the curriculum and felt pride in his accomplishment, but both he and his wife, Alice, desperately missed Napa Valley. In 1961 Leon Brendel's winery and small acreage near St. Helena became available, so the Heitzes bought the property, moved back to the valley, and established Heitz Cellars. Since the Brendel property was planted solely with Grignolino grapevines, Heitz expanded his inventory by purchasing Chardonnay and Pinot Noir from Sonoma's Hanzell Vineyards. Heitz noted that Hanzell aged its wines in French Limousin barrels. Joe, accustomed to American oak during his time at BV, liked the complexity that the French oak added to the wine. His customers agreed, so the Heitzes found it necessary to expand their production and storage capacity. In 1964 they purchased the Holt property on Taplin Road off the Silverado Trail that encompassed 160 acres of rocky soil, an old country house, and a beautiful stone winery built in 1898. The following year, the Heitzes' good friends Belle and Barney Rhodes sold their small vineyard and acreage in Oakville to an Ojai couple named Tom and Martha May. The Rhodeses left the young couple two bottles of Heitz champagne as a house-warming gift. Tom and Martha loved the wines and soon visited the Heitz winery to purchase some more. The couples began chatting, and Joe learned that the Mays had some Cabernet grapes for sale, their first crop from Martha's vineyard, but did not know what to do with them. "We'll crush them," Heitz said. He blended the Mays' inaugural '65 vintage with some of his own Cabernet and found the results pleasing. As an experiment, Joe decided to process the Mays' grapes separately the following harvest. "By a stroke of what turned out to be genius, but pure luck, we put the vineyard name 'Martha's Vineyard' on the [1966] label," Heitz said. His "Martha's Vineyard" Cabernet Sauvignon became Napa Valley's first vineyard-designated wine, earned rave reviews from wine critics, and became an instant cult classic.[11]

Heitz also set the stage for another one of André's mentoring success stories when Joe discovered Theo Rosenbrand. Theo and his wife Paula immigrated to America from Holland in December 1954. Upon their arrival, the Rosenbrands headed west to visit Theo's friend Anton Krist, the head gardener at Beaulieu Vineyard in Rutherford. On Christmas Eve, the Dutch couple disembarked from a Greyhound bus and, as prearranged by Krist, spent the night in one of the de Pins family's guest rooms. The following morning, the Rosenbrands stood on their balcony, admiring Madame's beautiful gardens, when they spotted a small man waving to them from down below. They did not realize it at the time, but it was their first glimpse of André Tchelistcheff. Later that morning, André's assistant Joe Heitz and his wife, Alice, stopped by to greet the Rosenbrands. The encounter made a strong impression on both couples, and they quickly became friends. After their brief stopover in Rutherford, Theo and Paula settled in Calistoga. He found work making copies of antiques, and Paula, with an assist from Heitz, landed a secretarial position at BV. In July 1956, Joe notified Theo about a cellar position that was opening up at BV. Rosenbrand decided to apply, interviewed with André, and got a job, as he put it, "dragging hoses" and "washing barrels." From his earliest encounters with André, Theo marveled at Tchelistcheff's tenacity, energy, and agility. He once witnessed André, loosened by a couple of glasses of wine, perform an "amazing" Cossack dance at a cellar party! Although the two argued repeatedly, they always reconciled, as André affectionately referred to the younger cellar worker as "Sonny" and Theo called his boss "Dad." Theo thought André's most admirable trait was his respect for everyone, especially the ordinary winery workers who pruned vines or washed barrels. André "valued . . . everybody that worked in the winery or in the fields," Rosenbrand said. "He didn't look down on [anyone]." Theo worked with Tchelistcheff from 1956 until André's retirement from BV in 1973. André appointed Rosenbrand as the cellar foreman in 1964, and BV hired Theo as its head winemaker from 1973 to 1979. "All that I know about wine and winemaking," Theo said, "has come out of André Tchelistcheff."[12]

When Paula Rosenbrand became pregnant with the couple's first child in July 1958, a young woman from St. Helena named Dorothy Andrew replaced her. Dorothy grew up in California's Central Valley during the Great Depression. Hoping to become a nurse, Dorothy completed nurse's training at San Diego's naval hospital in the 1940s, but marriage and the birth of four children derailed those plans. In 1958 the Andrews moved from the Sierra foothills to St. Helena, where Dorothy's husband, Oberlym, became the inaugural principal of the Robert Louis Stevenson School. At first Dorothy worked part-time at the high school and volunteered with the Cub Scouts, Girl Scouts, 4-H, and the Rainbow Girls. When she joined Beaulieu as a full-time employee in 1958, Dorothy served as the winery's only secretary. She worked seven days a week during the harvest and crush, and became indispensable during spring frosts. On those frigid nights, Dorothy called the workers to the vineyards and brought coffee and sandwiches to their various smudge-pot stations between 10 p.m. and 6 a.m. Theo Rosenbrand recalled one particularly bad spring frost in the 1960s that lasted twenty-one consecutive nights. André served as one of Dorothy's bosses and lived only several houses down the street from the Andrew family on Sulphur Springs Avenue in St. Helena. Dorothy's daughters even babysat for André's grandson, Paul, who moved in with the Tchelistcheffs following Dimitri's divorce. At first, Dorothy felt intimidated by Tchelistcheff, but soon she became intrigued by André's charm, wit, and sophistication. By the late 1960s, it became increasingly clear that André had developed a similar fascination for Dorothy Andrew.[13]

Over the course of his career at Beaulieu, André's roles evolved from head enologist-viticulturist to technical director and then to one of BV's vice presidents. André's skillful winemaking artistry helped position BV for continued prosperity in the 1950s and 1960s, complemented by the marketing achievements of Aldo Fabbrini and Legh Knowles. Fabbrini began managing BV after the war, replacing his brother Nino, who died in 1946. Like his brother, Aldo continued placing Beaulieu wines on high-profile restaurant and hotel wine lists, and maintained BV's unofficial status as the winery of state. The Georges de Latour Private Reserve appeared with regularity at White House dinners and was served to foreign dignitaries at formal State Department events. BV's production increased from sixty-five thousand to eighty-five thousand cases between 1959 and 1962, another clear indicator of its success. Taking advantage of the uptick in premium wine sales in the late 1950s, Beaulieu joined Inglenook, Krug, Beringer, and Martini to form the California Premium Wine Association. The new consortium pledged to work cooperatively to further the cause of wine for "real wine users." Nationally, table wine sales continued to lag behind fortified wines such as port, brandy, and muscatel, but the trend started shifting by the 1960s. After World War II, increasing numbers of Americans traveled abroad, experiencing Old World wine culture for the first time. Promotional literature in the 1950s such as John Melville's *Guide to California Wines* and Leon Adams's *Commonsense Book of Wine* also helped to popularize California's premium wine producers and demystify the wine experience. Most important, the quality and quantity of premium table wines took off in postwar America. The tipping point came in 1967: for the first time since the repeal of Prohibition, sales of table wine surpassed those of its fortified competitor.[14]

When Fabbrini retired in 1962, BV replaced Aldo with Legh Knowles, a self-described "iconoclastic maverick." Born in 1919 in Danbury, Connecticut, Knowles grew up in a family of hatters who immigrated to America from England. Legh's father, who always wanted to be a trumpeter rather than a hatter, purchased a trumpet for Legh when the boy was eight. While visiting his local speakeasy, the elder Knowles met a British Army deserter named Bill Dalton and discovered that he offered trumpet lessons. Under Dalton's tutelage, Legh's trumpet career blossomed quickly. By the age of twelve, Legh started playing on the nightclub circuit in Connecticut and Pennsylvania. In 1938 Knowles joined the Glenn Miller Orchestra and toured the country for the next two years, playing virtually nonstop. During this period, Legh helped make 123 records with Miller's band, including such hits as "In the Mood," "Moonlight Serenade," and "Tuxedo Junction." Knowles enlisted in the U.S. Army Air Forces at the outset of World War II and after the war became a member of the Wine Advisory Board in Washington DC. "I didn't know anything about wine, but they wanted someone who could stand up before large crowds and I'd done a lot of that." Knowles later became a salesman for the E. & J. Gallo wine empire in Modesto but became frustrated with the Gallos' reluctance to enter the premium wine market. As a result, Knowles landed a managerial position at BV and worked at Beaulieu for the next twenty-seven years as its president and chairman. Legh greatly admired the marquis and marquise de Pins, and regarded André as "so warm and so great. André used to just make sure the grapes were planted in the right place." Knowles also worked with André to "compact the line." When Legh started at BV, the winery distributed forty different wine varietals. André spent years urging Beaulieu's owners to concentrate their production. "I am producing little starlets when I should produce only great stars," André once said. With his help, Knowles managed to compact BV's distribution to eight varietals and to focus much more of Beaulieu's production in Cabernet Sauvignon.[15]

Two and a half years prior to Knowles's arrival at Beaulieu, André hired a new assistant enologist who would sustain Tchelistcheff's track record of mentoring success. Miljenko (Mike) Grgich, attracted by the winery's elite status as well as André's cosmopolitan background, joined Beaulieu in November 1959. Born in Croatia (part of Yugoslavia) in 1923 as the youngest of eleven children, Grgich grew up on a farm.

He remembered stomping grapes at the age of three and working as a shepherd beginning at age six. After World War II, Grgich studied enology and viticulture at the University of Zagreb, graduating in 1954. Like Tchelistcheff, Grgich was exposed to an expansive curriculum that included chemistry, physics, mathematics, biology, genetics, botany, microbiology, and agronomy. Mike's favorite professor, Marko Mohaček, taught chemistry, loved his students, and shared his expertise in wine. Two months prior to Mohaček's retirement, Yugoslavia's communist government laid him off, thwarting his access to full retirement benefits. Grgich complained to the dean, and after that "the secret police started to follow me around," Grgich said. "I was very much in danger, and I was scared to death." To avoid possible arrest, he traveled to West Germany in 1954, worked on a farm as an exchange student, and obtained a Canadian visa in 1956.[16]

Grgich settled in British Columbia and spent the next two years washing dishes and waiting tables at Vancouver College. Mike found Canada's progressive spirit inspiring, but he aspired to move to the United States and work in California's wine industry. In 1958 he applied for and landed a position at Napa Valley's Souverain winery, working for winemaker Lee Stewart. Another André protégé, Stewart impressed the young Croatian immigrant with his high standards and prodigious work ethic. Mike worked for Stewart for four months during the crush and spent the next year in the champagne department at Christian Brothers winery in St. Helena. "On one of my days off I went to see André Tchelistcheff," Grgich said, "and told him I was looking for a better job." André took his name and about one month later called to offer Mike a position in BV's lab. During his first several months at Beaulieu, Grgich struggled to learn the winery's protocols and regularly put in twelve-hour days. André told Grgich, "I know that you are not experienced, but I'll give you two months. If you make it in two months you'll stay. If you don't make it, don't blame me." After two months of steady progress, Grgich erased any doubts about his competency. André not only retained Grgich but also awarded him a twenty-five cent raise.[17]

Grgich's role at Beaulieu Vineyard evolved from wine chemist to quality control manager. According to Mike, "Quality control means to control the grapes in the vineyard, to control when to pick them and when to crush them, when they are fermenting, when they are being fined, racked, bottled—all the way through." André told Mike again and again that he needed to serve as Tchelistcheff's "eyes," or the one person André could trust to provide reliable information on daily operations in the winery and the vineyards. Meanwhile, André never stopped experimenting. For example, in the early 1960s, Tchelistcheff tested frost protection techniques that began with burning tires and bales of hay; then he transitioned to smudge pots and wind machines. Grgich recalled working in the winery by day and the vineyards during the night, "running around like a rabbit from thermometer to thermometer, measuring temperature in order to know when to light smudge pots and start the machines." Working with Grgich, André also established a systematic micro-filtering approach to bottling using Millipore filters. In addition, BV became the first winery in California to induce malolactic fermentation in all of its red wines. Mike remembered accompanying André in the 1960s to a symposium at UC-Davis, where Tchelistcheff lectured graduate students and faculty on the principles of malolactic fermentation. Despite all of Tchelistcheff's technical achievements, Grgich still regarded André as more of a viticulturist than a winemaker. "But, you know," Grgich reflected, "André worked at a time when there were not many other quality winemakers. André Tchelistcheff made superior wines in those days because nobody else knew how to do it better."[18]

Grgich participated regularly in Tchelistcheff's monthly Napa Valley Wine Technical Group meetings and learned a great deal from André and his impressive cohort. According to Mike, the group's monthly gatherings in those days focused its discussions on how to make better wine, paying much less attention to the industry's later obsession with marketing, promotion, and hospitality. André played a central role in this qualitative approach to winemaking, in Grgich's opinion. "I was very fortunate to meet with André Tchelistcheff at Beaulieu Vineyard, and even more fortunate that I was accepted to work for him," Mike said. He believed that André created the most "academically-oriented" winery in Napa Valley and that André's taste surpassed that of any of his peers, Grgich also admired André's strict devotion to his craft and marveled at his ability to produce the best Cabernets in the United States year after year on such a limited budget. Mike believed that all of the accolades heaped upon André over his lifetime were not only well deserved but also the direct result of André's success in bridging his experiences in Russia, Czechoslovakia, Bulgaria, Yugoslavia, and France with the winemaking traditions of California. André "brought to California not only the spirit of the high quality of wines and good taste," Grgich observed, "but he [also] brought authority into wine-making." Yet despite all of his success, André eschewed pretense and felt most at home not in the winery but in the vineyards. Grgich said that on many occasions he "had to go to pull [André] from the vineyard to come and taste wine. [André] was very close to Mother Nature."[19]

In 1968 Grgich joined Robert Mondavi's two-year-old winery in Oakville, serving as the winemaker there until 1972. Bob started his own winery after a bitter, intra-family fracas led to his expulsion from Charles Krug. For twenty-three years, the Mondavi brothers ran a successful operation at Krug but increasingly disagreed on its future direction. Unlike his more conservative brother, Bob wanted to invest more heavily in the latest winemaking technologies and to expand the winery's promotional efforts nationally and internationally. Eventually, sibling tensions exploded over the purchase of a $2,500 mink coat. Bob bought the garment in 1963 from San Francisco's exclusive I. Magnin and Company for his wife, Marjorie, to wear at a White House dinner. The event, postponed after President John F. Kennedy's assassination in November 1963, was eventually hosted by President Lyndon Johnson and his wife, Lady Bird. Afterward, on a chilly autumn morning in 1965, Peter berated his brother for purchasing the coat and accused Bob of essentially stealing the funds from their company's expense account.

Peter's accusation prompted a physical altercation between the brothers that included fisticuffs, wrestling, choking, and substantial cursing. The fallout was severe. Led by the Mondavi matriarch, Rosa, most of the family rallied behind Peter and voted to oust Bob from Charles Krug in 1965. Jobless and nearly broke, Bob found investors, acquired acreage in C. W. Crabb's historic To-Kalon vineyard in Oakville, and started his own winery one year later. To avenge his ignominious dismissal from Krug, Mondavi even changed the pronunciation of his family name from mon-DAY-vee to mon-DAH-vee.[20]

Grgich made the move to the Robert Mondavi winery because he considered André's son, Dimitri, to be André's natural successor at BV. Grgich brought with him the techniques he had learned from André, including malolactic fermentation, and started making superior Cabernets. Since Mike had more freedom to experiment at Mondavi, "I really blossomed there," Grgich said. In fact, he regarded his '69 Robert Mondavi Cabernet Sauvignon as the best wine he ever made. In 1972 Jim Barrett and Ernie Hahn purchased the Chateau Montelena Winery north of Calistoga and began looking for a winemaker. Barrett, cognizant of Mike's winemaking pedigree, approached Grgich and offered him a position as winemaker, vineyardist, and limited partner. Mike calculated that with Mondavi's two sons in front of him, much like his previous situation at Beaulieu, he needed to accept Barrett's offer. Grgich started at Chateau Montelena in May 1972 and needed to piece together enough equipment to make wine by September. "I put my body and soul into producing my first wine there, a '72 Chardonnay," Grgich said. His Chateau Montelena '72 is still regarded as one of the best Chardonnays ever produced in California and is often compared to that of Burgundy's famous Bâtard-Montrachet Grand Cru. The following year Grgich produced another excellent Chardonnay, which he considered the third-best wine of his winemaking career, and it triumphed over France's greatest whites at a tasting in Paris in 1976.[21]

In 1964, during Grgich's tenure at Beaulieu Vineyard, a thirty-five-year-old political scientist from Chicago named Warren Winiarski joined André's monthly Napa Valley Wine Technical Group meetings. From his extensive readings on Napa Valley's modern wine history, Winiarski recognized most of the group's vintners but did not know and had never met Tchelistcheff. As Winiarski explained it, André had remained off his radar because, unlike the rest of the group's members, André never owned a winery. Warren could not understand "how this man of such remarkable skills never sought himself to become an entrepreneur." Nevertheless, Winiarski quickly learned about Tchelistcheff and became one of his principal devotees. Winiarski marveled at what he described as André's "Cartesian" duality: to Warren, André embodied the "spirit of geometry" and the "spirit of finesse." According to Winiarski, Tchelistcheff's approach to winemaking combined the classical, orderly, organized, coherent, and scientific with the intuitional, free spirited, free formed, and novel. André once told Warren, "There are really no rules in winemaking, except the rule that there is no rule." At times impish and mischievous, Tchelistcheff could also be an "extraordinarily hard disciplinarian," Winiarski said. In his opinion, André's poetic sensibility and iron discipline made him special. As a result, when Winiarski opened his own winery in 1970, the first consultant he approached was André Tchelistcheff.[22]

Winiarski's journey to Napa Valley followed an unconventional route. Born in 1928 in Chicago, Illinois, Winiarski grew up in a cohesive Polish American family neighborhood. His Polish family name, Winiarski, means "son of a winemaker." Warren's father ran a livery business in Chicago, but he also made dandelion and fruit wines on the side that were served at social events for other Polish American families. Winiarski attended a public high school in Chicago, briefly attended the University of Chicago, and earned his baccalaureate from St. John's College in Annapolis, Maryland. Following graduation, he returned to his hometown and enrolled in a master's degree program in political science at the University of Chicago. During this period, he also studied at the University of Florence in Italy, where he worked on the Machiavelli manuscripts at the Laurentian Library. By the

87

time Warren received his degree, he was married, raising a family, and teaching at the University of Chicago. His appreciation for wine had blossomed during his studies in Italy and reached an "epiphanal" moment during his sixth year of teaching in Chicago, one that dramatically changed his career trajectory. "It's been my experience that everyone who is engaged with wine in a more than casual way has some experience in which wine reveals itself for the first time, no matter how many times you've had it before and under what circumstances," Winiarski once observed. His epiphany took place during a meal that featured a special wine brought by a family friend. At that moment, Winiarski said, the possibility of becoming a winemaker "illuminated itself in a way it had never appeared before."[23]

Winiarski's exploratory journey into the winemaking world started in New Mexico, where he traveled alone in the early 1960s to learn about opportunities in grape growing and apple production in the Rio Grande River valley. Motoring by day in his station wagon, sleeping in the back at night, Winiarski discovered some impressive farms in the valley. Once outside of the irrigated region, however, Warren encountered a godforsaken, arid countryside. He remembered stopping by an abandoned adobe house that he said "had an air of desolation [with] tumbleweeds rolling across my field of vision." At that moment, a voice in Warren's head told him that his ancestors would curse him for eternity for giving up everything to move to such a wretched place. He returned to Chicago and started working on his plan B. He read every reliable wine book available, with two standing out in particular: Philip Wagner's *Grapes into Wine: The Art of Making Wine in America* and John Storm's *An Invitation to Wine*, which focused on California and some of the smaller wineries in the state. He also wrote to the famous UC-Davis enologist Maynard Amerine, who suggested that Warren contact Lee Stewart at Souverain in the Napa Valley. Winiarski followed up, landed a job with Stewart in 1964, and became part of a two-man team doing, in Warren's words, "everything and anything."[24]

Lee Stewart worked as a sales executive for Armour and Company before retiring in 1943 at the age of forty-eight. He purchased thirty acres and the old Rossini Winery on Napa Valley's Howell Mountain the same year, yielded his first harvest in 1944, and named his new winery Souverain. Yet another André protégé, Stewart learned most of his winemaking skills from Tchelistcheff and became known for clean winemaking practices, a commitment to innovation, and steadfast precision. Winiarski described Stewart as a "man of extremely fastidious characteristics, obsessively concerned with the minutiae and the detail and the cleanliness of all the process." As a result, Stewart's wines garnered numerous awards, winning ninety-three medals at the California State Fair over a ten-year period. After working for Stewart for two years, Winiarski reasoned that it takes two crushes to learn the essentials of winemaking. Looking to advance his career, Winiarski talked to Stewart about leaving, and "we both agreed that it was the very best thing that could have happened," Warren said. After parting ways with Souverain, Winiarski sought André's advice. André encouraged him to talk to Ivan Schoch, one of the partners in Robert Mondavi's new winery in Oakville. Winiarski successfully interviewed with Ivan and Bob, and became the Mondavi Winery's new winemaker prior to its first crush in 1966. He stayed for two cycles, per Winiarski's fundamental philosophy; left in 1968; and spent the next two years consulting for wineries in Sonoma and Mendocino Counties.[25]

During the 1960s, Winiarski also took short courses at UC-Davis and read constantly. He kept studying to master the sequence and matrix for producing quality wine and, more important, to understand why he was doing it. "Sometimes I would ask a key question, and a short, simple answer would illuminate a complex whole without a long explanation," he said. "This whole picture was emerging." Winiarski also continued searching for property in Napa Valley. In 1970 he discovered Stag's Leap Vineyard, forty acres previously owned by Nathan Fay, and formed an investment group to purchase it. Winiarski planted Cabernet Sauvignon and Merlot, and built a winery—Stag's Leap

Wine Cellars—three years later. Winiarski wanted to hire André as his consultant, and eventually he did, but in 1970 BV's management would not permit it. The year before, André's circumstances at Beaulieu Vineyard had changed dramatically, requiring yet another strategic adjustment by the Russian émigré. Meanwhile, Winiarski went on to produce a 1973 Cabernet in his second crush at Stag's Leap that scored a stunning victory in a Paris tasting, rocketing its winemaker and his winery into worldwide fame.[26]

CHAPTER 6

Heublein

Paradoxically, the big corporations display the worst
parochialism. They refer all decisions, important and
otherwise, back to the home office, and impose on the
valley the true ineptitude of the corporate citizen. . . .
They have poisoned the well for everyone.

—ANONYMOUS

In 1962 André finally convinced Madame de Pins to invest in a rare
winery upgrade. Typically she rejected André's requests out of hand.
"How come, Mr. Tchelistcheff?" she often replied. "My father told me
that he left me in perfect shape," meaning debt free and "not a penny
owed to any bank." Nonetheless, for years Tchelistcheff dreamed of
acquiring a cool-climate vineyard, one suitable for Burgundian varietals
such as Pinot Noir and Chardonnay in contrast to Rutherford's more
favorable Bordeaux microclimate. As André once said, many Napa
Valley vintners erred in believing that they could "build a reputation of
Burgundy and Bordeaux and Sauternes within the same geographical
area, within the same soil. There must be something wrong with [these]
people," André surmised. André and his good friend Louis P. Martini
believed that the Carneros district, situated along the southern fringes
of Napa and Sonoma Counties and adjacent to San Pablo Bay, featured
a Burgundian terroir par excellence. For once Madame reluctantly
agreed with André and secured a bank loan, something her father

would never do, to purchase 160 acres in Los Carneros. The property became BV Ranch Number 5. After the purchase, Hélène spoke at a public event, proclaiming that "André Tchelistcheff is my great friend, but the most costly friend I've had in my life!" Partly true, yet by the 1960s André recognized that to remain competitive BV needed to make major capital upgrades—stainless steel tanks to replace antiquated redwood casks and new refrigeration units, pumps, bottling machinery, and a receiving station—all of which, André observed, had the potential of "choking the family." André likened a major winery such as Beaulieu to a shark, "continuously asking for more and more fish to be fed." Two years after Beaulieu's purchase of its Carneros property, a new breed of shark swallowed BV's neighborhood rival, temporarily transforming one of Napa Valley's most distinguished châteaus into a parody of its former self.[1]

United Vintners, managed by Louis Petri and Larry Solari, purchased John Daniel's beloved Inglenook winery in 1964 for $1.2 million. News of the sale sent shock waves throughout the valley. Daniel, the grandnephew of Gustave Niebaum, had kept alive his granduncle's legacy since the repeal of Prohibition; so why sell a family treasure to a large cooperative like United Vintners, known principally for its bulk wines sourced from Central Valley grapes? John and his sister, Suzanne, grew up in Gustave's beautiful Victorian mansion on Rutherford's Inglenook estate and were raised by Gustave's widow, Susan. During Prohibition, Susan felt duty bound to maintain the surrounding vineyards and at repeal decided to reactivate the Inglenook cellar. John returned to the estate in 1933 after completing an engineering degree at Stanford, became joint owner with his sister when his grandaunt died in 1936, and thrust himself into the wine business. Working with wine men Carl Bundschu and George Deuer, Daniel helped resurrect Inglenook into one of Napa Valley's finest wineries between 1933 and 1964. Daniel succeeded by adhering to the exacting standards of his granduncle, who insisted that only the best wines could be sold under the Inglenook label. As a result, Daniel refused to bottle substandard vintages and instead sold those wines in bulk without labeling it. Tchelistcheff deeply respected his high standards and qualitative approach to wine distribution. "We, Beaulieu, which was fed by the business, never was able to eliminate a vintage," André said.[2]

Industry experts and consumers alike appreciated Inglenook's impeccable standards as well, as its wines remained in high demand during Daniel's era of ownership. Yet John's meticulous approach also meant that his winery almost never turned a profit. In addition, by the 1960s his winery required major technical upgrades, mirroring Beaulieu's plight. Compounding these financial considerations, Daniel had to contend with a tumultuous domestic life. His wife, Betty, a nominal Mormon, hated his winery and regarded wine as evil. According to author James Conaway, her erratic behavior, domineering personality, and predilection for extramarital affairs weighed heavily on Daniel, who struggled to maintain his dignity and gentlemanly manner. In addition to these concerns, Inglenook's winemaker George Deuer, who worked side by side with Daniel for a quarter century, announced his plan to retire. As a result, when Louis Petri and Larry Solari expressed interest in purchasing Inglenook in early 1964, Daniel decided to act. Petri owned United Vintners, the largest wine producer in California in the mid-1960s, with brands that included Italian Swiss Colony. Petri also helped organize Allied Grape Growers, a cooperative with vineyards in the Central Valley and Sonoma County, that represented the parent company of United Vintners. Petri served as chief executive officer of United Vintners, a sales and marketing vehicle for Allied Grape Growers, and appointed Larry Solari as its chairman. Both men promised to maintain Inglenook's sterling reputation, selling only varietal wines rather than cheap generics. Solari called Inglenook the "Tiffany of the California wine industry." Despite these promises, valley insiders worried about what the sale of Inglenook represented for the future of Napa Valley. In the words of James Conaway, "At best, John had handed over the keys to a couple of promoters. At worst, he had let the barbarians into the valley."[3]

One year after the purchase, Petri and Solari moved Inglenook's winemaking production to a central plant in Oakville and used the Rutherford property for storage and promotion. Solari also began marketing "rivers" of Inglenook "generic vintage dated" wines that sourced their grapes from the Central Valley. Solari's profit-making approach, emphasizing quantity over quality, began blurring the brand's distinction between Inglenook's estate-farmed treasures with its cheap, mass-produced generics. As sales of Inglenook-labeled wines soared, United Vintners began looking for opportunities to sell off its assets, which included the Inglenook brand, for a considerable profit. In 1969 Heublein, a beverage and food products giant headquartered in Hartford, Connecticut, learned from an industry analyst in San Francisco that United Vintners and its parent company, Allied Grape Growers, might be up for sale. Seeking to reduce Heublein's over-reliance on vodka production, which represented three-quarters of its corporate sales, Heublein's executives saw an opportunity. The company distributed products such as Harvey's Bristol Cream sherry and Lancers rosé, which were popular and profitable but prosaic. A table wine consortium that included the prestigious Inglenook brand might transform Heublein's reputation, potentially casting it as the purveyor of superior wines. Its chief executive officer, Stuart Watson, dispatched twenty-nine-year-old Andy Beckstoffer to Napa Valley to negotiate with Petri and Solari. A Virginia native and recent graduate of Dartmouth College's Amos Tuck School of Business, Beckstoffer served as Heublein's director of acquisition analysis. Brash, articulate, and driven, Beckstoffer began a journey west that eventually proved highly profitable for himself, if not Heublein.[4]

Beckstoffer met with Solari at his home north of St. Helena and made a sales pitch. He argued that Heublein was in a much better position than Allied Vintners, the production and marketing vehicle for Allied Grape Growers, to promote and market its wines. "You guys have the grapes and brands," Beckstoffer said, and "we have the cash and marketing expertise. Let us carry you into the new world."

United Vintners, looking to unload a surplus of grapes at a considerable profit, went for the deal. Heublein paid Allied $32 million for the Inglenook brand and an additional $65 million for Allied's inventory. Known primarily for its sales of Smirnoff vodka, a superlative value-added commodity, Heublein now looked to profit from its Napa Valley investment. Using grapes from hundreds of Allied growers not even remotely associated with the Rutherford property, Heublein cashed in on the Inglenook brand by labeling all of its wines "estate bottled." One of them was a half-gallon jug wine called Navalle, named after the creek that ran through the old Niebaum estate. Daniel originally introduced Navalle as a secondary label and distributed no more than five thousand cases annually. Under Heublein, Navalle and other Inglenook-labeled generics reached eight million cases per year. For many consumers, the Inglenook brand soon became synonymous with cheap jug wine, prompting one wine critic to write that "Inglenook jumped from prestige to plonk" almost overnight. After the original sale of Inglenook to United Vintners in 1964, John Daniel stayed on as a consultant but grew disillusioned and decided to retire in 1966. Heartbroken and depressed, Daniel continued to remain active in Napa's leading viticultural organizations and spearheaded an unsuccessful effort to block the establishment of an agricultural preserve on the valley floor in 1968. Heublein's acquisition of Inglenook the following year put him over the edge. In July 1970, Daniel reportedly suffered a fatal heart attack in his family home at the age of sixty-three. In the words of historian Charles Sullivan, "John Daniel's death in 1970 seemed an unhappy coda to the demise of a great Napa institution."[5]

After the stunning sale of Inglenook, the second event to rock Napa Valley in the late 1960s involved André Tchelistcheff, then aged sixty-seven, and Dorothy Andrew, who was forty-four. As Dorothy later characterized it, in 1968 "I got a divorce and he got a divorce, and St. Helena tipped on its side." Why did it happen? To outside observers, André's marriage to his first wife, Catherine, had deteriorated over time. Catherine, introverted and withdrawn, never fully adjusted to rural

California. "She was a very reticent woman," Dagmar Sullivan observed, and "didn't like people very much." Catherine seemed close to her son, Dimitri, and grandson, Paul, whom she and André raised in their St. Helena home, but she refrained from socializing. In Dagmar's opinion, André "was very sad with his first wife. They got along like *discontinué*, as the French would say." In contrast, André, who was extroverted, charming, and cosmopolitan, discovered in Dorothy a kindred spirit. Unlike Catherine, Dorothy exuded warmth and sociability, loved to travel, and had a wonderful sense of humor. Like André, Dorothy also experienced her own personal challenges in the 1960s, including the tragic death of her youngest son in 1962 and frequent separations from her first husband, who was often deployed to Travis Air Force Base near Fairfield, California, during the Vietnam War era. Whatever the possible reasons for divorcing their spouses, the fact remains that André and Dorothy fell in love. As a result, they chose to chart a new course and take the bold step of remarrying.[6]

According to Barbara Stone, Dorothy's younger daughter, the turning point in their transition to a new life together happened one day in the St. Helena Public Cemetery. Dorothy went there by herself to visit her son's grave. When she arrived, Dorothy heard someone weeping and turned around to discover André. He approached her and "poured out his heart to her . . . and [told her] she was just wonderful and he couldn't stand the hurt that she was going through," Barbara said. "He just got *real* emotional." In Barbara's words, "It was hook, line, and sinker" for her mother. "And he became her *strength*," Barbara said. In the winter of 1968, Dorothy accompanied André to Paris, her first overseas trip. They stayed in a charming hotel on the Rue de Rennes near Montparnasse, took in all of the familiar sites, and visited wineries where André never failed to impress his hosts. Later that spring, Dorothy drove her Volkswagen to Northern California to collect Barbara, who had just finished her first year at California State University–Chico. Dorothy advised Barbara that she no longer resided in their St. Helena home. "Oh. Are you going to live at Travis with Dad?" Barbara asked. "No," Dorothy said, "I'm going to marry Mr. Tchelistcheff."[7]

The news floored Barbara and stunned valley residents. Dagmar Sullivan spent the summer of '68 in the valley and recalled that "everybody was talking about it." Skeptical of the new arrangement at first, Dorothy's children came to accept their mother's decision and even began to think of André as their surrogate father. Barbara felt much closer to André than to her own father, who seemed disinterested in her life choices to the point of not even caring about which college she attended. The girls began calling André *Deda*, an endearing term meaning "grandfather" in Russian. Dorothy's elder daughter, Susan Merle, observed that "Deda was supportive of Mother and saw to it that she saw us or that she maintained some contact with us as much as possible." According to Susan, "André was always there. . . . And you really felt comfortable at any time talking to him. And he treated us like we were his children as well." Dorothy later observed, "[André] understood [my] children better than I did. My two girls would . . . just consult him on anything. But he understood [them]. And he understood their problems."[8]

Dagmar Sullivan observed that André lightened up after his marriage to Dorothy and seemed much happier than before. Rob Davis, one of André's star winemaking pupils, believed that Dorothy's companionship lengthened André's life by a considerable margin. André and Dorothy bought a modest single-story home in Napa and lived comfortably yet unpretentiously. Despite André's fame as a winemaker, he did not bother to collect wine; the Tchelistcheffs' wine "cellar" consisted of a few bottles stored under their bed. As André once said, "Some people drink wine and some people are librarians." When not at work, gardening was his favorite domestic pastime. "He loved to grow things," Dorothy said. "I used to think I'd have to [put] dirt . . . on the roof so he could plant something." She watched his diet and prepared healthful evening meals followed by his favorite after-dinner drink, tea sweetened with jam. Not much of a cook himself, André once volunteered to make his own coffee and asked Dorothy how many beans he should boil.[9]

Dorothy also sustained Russian traditions of significance to André, most notably the blini gatherings and Russian Easter celebrations. At the Tchelistcheffs' annual spring blini parties, Dorothy prepared exquisite Russian blinis, which were accompanied by various types of fish, caviar, chopped eggs, melted butter, sour cream, champagne, and, of course, vodka. The couple invited senior wine professionals, family members, and junior winemakers, all of whom intermingled at two tables set up in the couple's living room. Jill Davis, another one of André's prized students, attended the Tchelistcheff blini gatherings regularly and always felt honored to be invited. "For those of us who were young, we were also learning how to be properly social. Sitting at a table where you did not know anyone, I felt like I grew up," Jill said. Dorothy also supported André's travels and accompanied him on most trips, including ones to France, Italy, and Washington State. Dorothy said that André especially loved visiting France, as "he always felt like he was home when we went to France." On one occasion Dorothy traveled alone to Australia to assist her daughter Barbara, who had moved to Sydney after college and given birth to twins. André anxiously awaited Dorothy's return and phoned his wife daily during her three-week absence. When she finally arrived home, she opened the front door to discover roses spread everywhere. "My God, André, I haven't died!" Dorothy exclaimed.[10]

The year 1968 proved to be momentous for André in other respects as well. After thirty years as an employee at Beaulieu Vineyard, Tchelistcheff decided that he wanted to "retire" and expand his consulting business. When he informed Madame de Pins of his decision, she insisted that André must first find and mentor a replacement. Dimitri seemed André's logical successor, but Tchelistcheff's son lacked his father's tolerance for the marquise's management style. Dimitri recommended Dick Peterson, one of his former colleagues at Gallo. Originally from Iowa, Peterson attended Iowa State University on a naval reserve officers training corps scholarship and graduated with a bachelor of science degree in chemical technology in 1952. After serving as an artillery officer in the Korean War, Peterson entered a graduate program in agricultural chemistry at UC-Berkeley from 1954 to 1958. Gallo, based in Modesto, hired Peterson in 1958 as a member of its technical staff. When Dimitri left Gallo in 1962, Peterson took over as the director of new product development. Dick remained in contact with Dimitri, and the two even considered purchasing a Napa Valley winery together in the mid-1960s. Since Peterson was a U.S. Army National Guard pilot, the two flew to Napa Valley from Stockton on weekends to scout for properties. They seriously considered purchasing Schramsberg Vineyard near Calistoga and coveted Freemark Abbey north of St. Helena, but they could not come up with the funding. During one of their winery-hunting expeditions, Peterson met Dimitri's father. The two hit it off, and Peterson recalls taking André on a short jaunt in his army plane from Rutherford to Calistoga and back.[11]

By 1967 Gallo surpassed Italian Swiss Colony to become the nation's biggest winery. Gallo led the industry in technology, grape tonnage crushed, and vineyard acreage, but it lacked what Peterson called the "snob" factor—the production of stylish table wines that transcended the taste and means of the average Gallo consumer. In December 1967, Peterson received a phone call from André, offering him a position at a winery reputed for its classic Cabernets instead of flavored pop wines and Thunderbird. "Dick, I put my finger on you," André said. "When can you transport your family to Beaulieu for the purpose of assuming the important position of enologist?" A few days later, Hélène de Pins invited Peterson to dinner in her San Francisco apartment and officially offered him the job. Thrilled by the prospect of working at such a legendary winery, Peterson accepted the position and agreed to begin on April 1, 1968.[12]

On the first of April, Peterson drove to Rutherford, met with André at 6 a.m., and began what became a weeklong tour of all five Beaulieu vineyards. André's first words to Peterson: "Bring a notebook. Take the notes." The tours lasted all morning, during which André described each vineyard's characteristics in intricate detail, block by block, row by row, and grape by grape. On their daily journeys, the two always stopped for coffee at Oakville Grocery around 8:30 a.m. and gossiped with many of Napa's other vineyard managers who regularly gathered there. "It surprised me how much André knew about vineyards," Peterson said. "I'd always known him to be a winemaker, but he always wanted to talk about the vineyards." At Beaulieu, Peterson believed that he "suddenly understood the French concept of 'winegrower,' which recognizes that each grape variety can produce different styles of wines depending on the methods of farming, the amount and timing of irrigation, ripeness level at harvest, and crop load on the vines." In Peterson's opinion, "André was a blue-ribbon winegrower par excellence."[13]

Dick also recalled an encounter at BV Ranch Number 3, when he asked André why Beaulieu planted so many grape varieties (eleven) in such a small space. André stopped the car and said, "My dear sir, when I first came here in 1938 there were *thirty-three* varieties in Ranch Number Three." That "shut me up," Dick said. André also introduced Peterson to each vineyard foreman and insisted that he also write down the names of their wives and kids. André "was family oriented and he knew them all well," Dick observed. Tchelistcheff also knew the twenty-five vineyard workers who lived in Mexico during the wintertime and had been traveling back to BV every spring for over two decades.[14]

During the vineyard tours, Peterson also learned about some of Madame de Pins's various quirks. When André told Dick that Madame insisted on using Private Reserve Cabernet Sauvignon from Beaulieu Ranch Number 1 to produce wine vinegar, Peterson was dumbstruck. "But André," Peterson interjected, "won't the flavor of Private Reserve Cabernet wine get totally lost under the pungent flavor of that vinegar?" André responded, "Well, my dear sir, perhaps for your taste that would be true—but for Madame's taste, only perfection is acceptable." He continued, "To use a lesser wine would be unthinkable." Tchelistcheff told Peterson that when Madame made the request for wine vinegar, Dick should "remove two barrels of Georges de Latour Private Reserve Cabernet Sauvignon from the winery aging cellar, and transport them to Madame's cellar number one, located closest to her country house. Then," André advised, "you will conduct the acetic acid fermentation, and turn that wine into the finest Private Reserve Cabernet Wine Vinegar." Incredulous, Peterson shook his head and carried on.[15]

After their morning vineyard tours, André and Dick returned to the winery and met with cellar foreman Theo Rosenbrand to chart the day's work schedule. In the afternoon, André, Dick, and Theo tasted and discussed various tank samples, a daily routine carried out for the rest of the year. Peterson marveled at Tchelistcheff's ability to produce superb wines year in and year out with "antiquated equipment held together with baling wire and glue." Coming from Gallo's much more advanced technical environment, Peterson found BV's substandard facilities—the lack of proper refrigeration and brass fittings, the open-top fermentation tanks, and the complete absence of stainless steel containers—appalling. It made little sense to Peterson that BV did not ferment white wine in stainless steel tanks. When he asked André specifically why Sauvignon Blanc was fermenting in redwood tanks, André responded, "Well, my dear sir, you show me the stainless steel tanks that I should ferment it in." He then told Dick to make a list of essential technical upgrades and present it to Madame de Pins. "She might listen to you because you are new. . . . I've been here thirty years and she doesn't listen to me anymore," André said. When Dick first raised the issue of stainless steel tanks with the marquise, she replied, "Oh, it seems to me André may have mentioned that to me once or twice before. I'm sure you are right." Months passed, accompanied by continual "prodding, pleading and pushing," until Madame finally granted Peterson the opportunity to make his case to Beaulieu's board of directors in May 1969. The following day, Madame de Pins called Peterson to her sitting room. Shaking her finger at him, Hélène told her new enologist, "Okay, Dick Peterson, you can install your damn stainless steel tanks, but I don't want anyone calling attention to them. I do not want any of the winery visitors to see them.... Now get out of here!"[16]

Madame de Pins had secured a bank loan earlier in the 1960s to purchase the Carneros property, and now she needed to take out an additional loan to purchase stainless steel tanks. The capitalization required to modernize her beloved winery must have weighed heavily on her, and most certainly it became a central topic of discussion in private family gatherings. More than anyone, André understood Madame's escalating anxieties. "Beaulieu Vineyard was a private family-owned company," André observed, "built with a tremendous amount of physical, mental, and moral effort by the founders—Georges de Latour and Fernande de Latour—with the sweat and risks and tremendous amount of economy." The de Latours had left their daughter, Hélène, a property "without one penny owed to a bank, without any debts, with . . . vineyards in the full production," André said. This heritage "remained settled, with the deep roots, in the mind of Madame de Pins." But the de Latour business model no longer worked in the economic and technical landscape of the 1960s. To remain competitive, the marquise needed to borrow money and most likely increasing amounts of it.[17]

Dagmar Sullivan's husband, Walter, a successful commercial real estate developer in San Francisco, took note of his mother-in-law's angst. He also paid close attention to Heublein's purchase of Inglenook and wondered if its executives might also be interested in acquiring Napa Valley's other most famous château. Without consulting either Dagmar or Hélène, Sullivan reached out to BV's attorney Ted Kolb to convey his family's possible interest in selling the winery. Sullivan urged Kolb to be discrete and refrain from leaking any word of the matter to his wife or the marquise until a deal could be reached. Kolb contacted Heublein's chief executive officer Stuart Watson and arranged a meeting to open discussions. Sullivan followed up by organizing a luncheon for Watson at the Beaulieu estate, ostensibly to acquaint Hélène and Dagmar with their new neighbor. Walter knew that the starstruck easterner would likely find the "beautiful place" overwhelming and thus become much more amenable to a negotiated deal. Of course, as James Conaway writes, Sullivan also "knew what the Heublein executives did not: that premium wineries were capital-intensive businesses that paid back nothing in the short run and sometimes nothing forever." Following Madame's characteristically sensational lunch, Sullivan took the Heublein executive on a garden tour, pulled Watson aside, and dropped the pretense. "If you make an unsolicited offer for Beaulieu," Sullivan said, "it will receive favorable consideration."[18]

Watson returned to Hartford and consulted with John Martin, chairman of the board, and Andy Beckstoffer, who had been recently promoted to vice president of planning. Martin did not object to the purchase, provided that the new property generate at least two million cases of wine annually. Beckstoffer expressed enthusiasm for the deal, especially given Beaulieu's profile, production statistics, and national distribution network. Watson was already sold and instructed Beckstoffer to meet with Sullivan and offer as much as $8 million for the BV brand, the winery and its inventory, its distributing partner, and its vineyards. Once the negotiations commenced in Ted Kolb's office in San Francisco, they went all day and into the early morning hours of the next. The end result was an agreement to sell BV to Heublein for $8.4 million. According to its terms, the de Pins family retained the family home and the original vineyard, BV Ranch Number 1, and Heublein acquired the rest. Several hours later, Walter broke the news to his mother-in-law and wife, desperately hoping they would be pleased and sign the contract willingly. Madame de Pins erupted, "How could you do this?" Dagmar simply began sobbing. Even years afterward, André said, "there were tears, tears, and tears." It took the women a week to come around to signing, and on June 5, 1969, the transaction was complete. Legh Knowles knew nothing about the sale until he received a call to meet the family in Ted Kolb's office. When he arrived, he found Madame and Dagmar in tears and Walter appearing sheepish. Knowles knew immediately what had happened, as he had spent the past several months fending off sales overtures from Anheuser-Busch, Bacardi, and Georgia-Pacific. In a remarkable turn of events, one of the greatest independent wineries in the country had just become another "piece of corporate property." "I did it. I sold out," the marquise told Knowles.[19]

André, the last major functionary at Beaulieu to find out about the sale, confronted Madame de Pins soon afterward. Dick Peterson overheard the argument, in which André opined that the winery, rather than cash, would have been a better legacy to her four grandchildren. "Listen, André," she said. "I have an obligation to my grandchildren [and] need to see that they have the good life that they deserve. The money will give them that." Despite her insistence, Hélène regretted the sale and remained distressed about it for the rest of her life. She soon realized that BV's assets had been seriously undervalued. In fact, selling Beaulieu, in the words of James Conaway, "was the worst business decision in the valley's history." In contrast, Andy Beckstoffer was in ecstasy and boasted right after the sale that "now we own Napa Valley." In one of his first assignments, Beckstoffer met with Tchelist-cheff to tout Beaulieu's new ownership and bring André on board. "And in my enthusiasm [I] told him all the wonders of Heublein and how we would bring money that the Madame didn't have," Beckstoffer recalled. André stood erect as always, maintained steady eye contact, and listened patiently to the silver-tongued Virginian. After a few moments, André responded, "Talk is cheap. We're going to see what you're going to do with the wines of Beaulieu."[20]

In the beginning, Heublein promised to maintain continuity in BV's organizational structure. Legh Knowles went from sales manager to general manager; Madame de Pins, at least theoretically, remained chair of the board; and André became vice president and technical director. At the initial meeting of Heublein executives and Beaulieu notables in San Francisco, Stuart Watson invited André to speak. André chose to take the high road and put a positive spin on the new arrangement. He praised Heublein for giving Beaulieu the possibility "to upgrade the quality of your fruit, which will give us the possibility to upgrade the quality of our wines, and the future is getting much brighter with the Heublein organization than it was before." At the dinner held at Trader Vic's following that meeting, Heublein board chairman John Martin addressed Madame de Pins and said, "Beaulieu remains a family organization because Heublein is a family organization." He invited the marquise to communicate with him directly should any problems arise on her end. It soon became apparent, however, that Martin's words rang hollow: Madame's position as board chair meant nothing because board meetings ceased to exist under Heublein's watch. "Beaulieu Vineyard as an independent organization died off within the next three months," André observed. "It was only beautiful words, only beautiful promises."[21]

Other troubling signs began to surface. Soon after the sale, Beckstoffer invited Dick Peterson to breakfast at Napa's Silverado Country Club. As their conversation progressed, Andy asked Dick why he was using Chenin Blanc grapes to make BV champagne. Assuming that Beckstoffer wanted Beaulieu to use higher-quality grapes for its sparkling wines, Peterson explained that BV typically used Chardonnay but needed all of those grapes for its Chardonnay table wine during the latest vintage. Beckstoffer frowned, shook his head, and said, "That's not what I mean." Andy told Peterson that Beaulieu should be using Thompson seedless grapes, which sold for $60 dollars per ton, instead of Chardonnay, which fetched $900. Primarily a raisin grape from the Central Valley, Thompson seedless had never before even registered in BV's wine universe. "Andy, there isn't anything you could say or do that would cause me to use Thompson in any BV wine," Peterson said. "Let's finish our breakfast and go away friends." "Dick, you'll never make a million dollars," Andy replied. Afterward Peterson related the encounter to André, who began referring to Beckstoffer as the "Thompson Seedless King."[22]

Two weeks after the Thompson seedless episode, a Heublein financial expert named Don Jackson arrived and met with BV's managers to present his business plan for Beaulieu. One month earlier, Jackson had met with Peterson to tour the winery and the vineyards. Dick had laid out an elaborate picture of each stage of winemaking, including vineyard management, harvesting, fermentation, bottling, warehousing, and aging. Jackson had appreciated the tutorial but reminded Peterson that Heublein's goal was to calculate the actual cost of the entire operation. "Just the costs, Dick, just the actual costs," Jackson insisted. When he returned with Heublein's business plan, he presented a chart that compared the production costs and return on investment of Cabernet Sauvignon and Gamay Beaujolais. He pointed out that Private Reserve Cabernet required four years of aging, whereas Gamay Beaujolais needed only six months to go from barrel to bottle and out the door for sale to the public. He also estimated that Cabernet cost nearly three times as much to produce, with a return on investment less than half of Gamay Beaujolais's potential. Jackson concluded that Beaulieu should dispense with its production of Private Reserve Cabernet Sauvignon, its principal mark of distinction for nearly a half century, and focus primarily on the far inferior, yet cheaper to produce, grape varietal Gamay Beaujolais. At first Beaulieu's managers thought Jackson was joking but soon realized he was serious. André and Dick remained speechless, completely dumbfounded by Jackson's preposterous proposal. Legh Knowles finally responded to Jackson: "Stuart Watson has told us that he intends for Beaulieu to grow from our present 150,000 cases per year to 500,000 cases. What makes you believe that Beaulieu could sell half a million cases of Gamay Beaujolais, *at any price?*" "Heublein is a marketing company," Jackson replied. It made no sense for Heublein to sell unprofitable products, Jackson argued. Instead, his company needed "to optimize profits by selling products that *do* make money."[23]

Legh's battle to save Private Reserve Cabernet paid off: when Heublein released its official Beaulieu Vineyards business analysis in January 1970, it did not mention eliminating Cabernet from the "product mix," but it implied that in future the company might need to buy its grapes rather than growing them given the high costs of farming. Peterson now realized that "winegrowing did not exist in [Heublein's] corporate mindset." Dick regarded it as an ominous sign, and it did not take long to reach fruition. At Beckstoffer's suggestion, Heublein created a vineyard management subsidiary called Vinifera Development Corporation. Heublein's executives put Beckstoffer in charge of Vinifera Development, giving him full control of managing the Inglenook and Beaulieu Vineyards and permission to purchase additional vineyard land in Napa and Mendocino Counties. Heublein made the move during the rise of one of the foremost agricultural labor movements of the era, the United Farm Workers (UFW). Led by Cesar Chavez, the UFW recruited a broad coalition of farm laborers in California, focusing initially on the San Joaquin Valley. Chavez rose to national prominence as a labor organizer during the 1960s and, by the end of the decade, had set his sights on the members of Central Valley's Allied Grape Growers, which was a major grape supplier of Heublein's United Vintners. Chavez wanted Heublein to pressure Allied to accept the UFW as its representative union in the Central Valley, and he threatened to boycott Heublein's products should it fail to deliver. Heublein's executives balked, the boycott ensued, and sales of Smirnoff vodka, Heublein's cash cow, began to suffer. Beckstoffer advised Heublein's executives to capitulate to Chavez's demands in the interest of "brand protection." "We promptly received an order from Heublein to unionize all our vineyard workers," Peterson said, despite that BV's Mexican laborers had voted 25–0 two weeks earlier not to unionize.[24]

Since the UFW required its workers to spend their weekends picketing Central Valley farms, most of Beaulieu's vineyard workers quit to find nonunion jobs elsewhere. André grew increasingly frustrated as he watched his beloved vineyards deteriorate. The UFW replacement workers, whom Peterson described as "a mob of ragged hippies," lacked their predecessors' work ethic and knew precious little about pruning vines. Having seen enough, André decided to retire in March 1970. Legh Knowles arranged a retirement dinner for André and Dorothy at Rutherford's El Real restaurant, during which André took Legh and Dick aside. "Legh," André said, "I predict that under Heublein's influence you will strangle this little baby Beaulieu with your own hands." When Heublein's executives learned about André's decision to retire, they pressured Knowles to keep him on as a consultant and sweetened the pot with a generous retirement package. André agreed to a three-year consulting contract that, according to Peterson, "gave André enough money and enough of a deal that it would more or less guarantee Dorothy's retirement, which André wanted very much." André still wondered whether Heublein's generous contract was essentially a public relations ploy. He soon found out.[25]

Looking to jettison its grape-growing business and all of the headaches that accompanied it, Heublein eventually sold Vinifera Development Corporation to Andy Beckstoffer. In a highly leveraged deal that included substantial loans from Heublein and the Connecticut Mutual Life Insurance Company, Beckstoffer positioned himself to become a future millionaire at the stroke of a pen. Beckstoffer now owned Beaulieu's and Inglenook's famous vineyards, including a significant portion of the To-Kalon vineyard in Oakville (BV Ranch Number 4), and later on became the owner of nearly nine hundred vineyard acres in Napa Valley (worth $350 million) and an additional twenty-seven hundred vineyard acres in Mendocino and Lake Counties.[26]

With Vinifera now in charge of Beaulieu's and Inglenook's vineyards, combined with Heublein's previous missteps, some sort of blowup seemed inevitable. Accounts vary on the identity of the individual, but one of Vinifera's vineyardists encountered André one day among the grapevines in the former BV Ranch Number 3. He shocked André by ordering him to *get out*, telling Beaulieu's former wine master that his presence in Vinifera's vineyards was no longer welcome. André went back to the winery in tears—Dorothy once said that the vineyards were like his children—and related his experience to Dick Peterson. André told Dick that it felt as if Vinifera had driven a wooden stake through his heart. Peterson, who regarded André as a second father, watched as his beleaguered mentor grew angrier and angrier. "Those goddamn bastards," André seethed. "Those goddamn bastards!"[27]

Soon thereafter, Andy Beckstoffer replaced Vinifera's existing vineyard manager with a young viticulturist from Fresno State named Bob Steinhauer. In mid-March 1971, Steinhauer arrived in Napa Valley and met with his boss, Beckstoffer, who instructed Bob to report to and take direction from Tchelistcheff. In light of André's previous experience with a Vinifera vineyardist, his first meeting with Bob did not go well. Bob recalled that André instructed him to get the truck and move the heaters to "BV-5." Steinhauer recalled asking André, "Where's the truck? Where's the heater? And where is BV-5?" André responded, "Unbelievable!" Several days later, the two met again, and this time Bob tried to gauge the reason for André's hostility. "Well, when you take the vineyards away from me, you cut my legs off. So why should I like you?" André asked. Steinhauer responded, "Well, I'm just here to learn from you." From that point forward, their relationship warmed. André tutored the young viticulturist on the characteristics of each vineyard, driving him around in Tchelistcheff's pickup. André also taught Bob to pay close attention to soil type and microclimate when planting new vines. "He was always teaching, always showing me things," Steinhauer said. Every afternoon Bob returned to the winery to get instructions for the following day. "André would put his arm around me . . . and take me into the back where he had a gallon of Muscat de Frontignan [hidden], and he would pour each one of us a glass of wine," Bob said. As the two sat there, sipping wine, André "would very quietly and gently tell me the things that I had done wrong, the things that I needed to do for the next day," Steinhauer recalled. André started calling Steinhauer "Bobby" and even invited him and his wife, Verna, to the Tchelistcheffs' home to celebrate Russian Easter that May. Steinhauer remembered that André, who seemed to be on a first-name basis with every employee at Beaulieu, always asked about Bob's family. "For me," Bob said, "[André] was a mentor and almost like a father."[28]

Like Steinhauer, Beckstoffer's admiration for André grew

exponentially over time. Andy later recognized that many of Heublein's early decisions "were driven by economic considerations" rather
than sound agricultural reasoning and that André kept Beckstoffer
grounded in reality. "I would ask him about things," Andy said, "because
I would have wild ideas. Remember, I wasn't a viticulturist." In particular, Beckstoffer gradually came to appreciate André's emphasis on
soil type as a fundamental prerequisite for growing superior grapes. At
one time, Andy placed climate first, soil second, and technique third
in his viticulture hierarchy. André's mentorship eventually convinced
Beckstoffer to consider soil type as paramount in the production of
great wines. "It was people like Tchelistcheff who were willing to put
up with guys like me," Andy pointed out, who elevated Napa wine
growing into world-class stature. "He was totally steeped in Napa
agriculture" and "never forgot that European orientation to the soil,
and never got to feel so important that he couldn't listen to the Bob
Steinhauers, that he couldn't accept the new ideas," Andy said.[29]

As André's relationship with Steinhauer gelled in 1971, the seventy-
year-old Tchelistcheff decided to purchase his first "fun" automobile, a
chrome-yellow Datsun 240Z sports car. Introduced to the American
market by Mr. K (Yutaka Katayama, president of Nissan Motors USA)
in 1970, the 240Z featured MacPherson struts, had rack-and-pinion
steering, and could reach a top speed of 125 miles per hour. André
loved his new coupe and drove it far and fast—often too fast. André
wrecked it three times over the next two decades. His third accident
was so serious, resulting in broken ribs and multiple lacerations, that
Dorothy took away his keys and never allowed her husband to drive
again. Nevertheless, André managed to rack up 240,000 miles on
his beloved 240Z before its ignominious transition into junkyard
wreckage.[30]

André continued his work as a BV consultant but chafed under some
of the contractual restrictions Heublein imposed on him, including
the provision that he could only consult with out-of-state wineries.
He also disapproved of Heublein's persistent efforts in pressuring

Legh Knowles to expand production. Heublein's executives could see no reason why BV should not increase its sales of Private Reserve, its most valuable wine, by a tenfold margin. Each time Stuart Watson raised the issue, Knowles carefully explained why it could not be done. Private Reserve Cabernet Sauvignon came from select vineyards that produced very special grapes, which were then carefully crafted into distinguished wines. Knowles once told them, "You can't sell eleven million Oldsmobiles and also eleven million Mercedes Benz." Of course, André agreed. Tchelistcheff had spent his entire career at Beaulieu producing "stylistically distinctive wines that showed the attributes of grape variety and vineyard site," the hallmark of BV's great Cabernets. Heublein's obsession with profit and scale threatened to place Beaulieu's winemakers in the unenviable position of making undistinguished, inoffensive, mass-produced *vin ordinaire*.[31]

The turning point for André came in early 1973. The *San Francisco Chronicle* published an interview with André in which he described his '46 Pinot Noir as the best Pinot he ever made but that its grapes were probably planted in the wrong place. André did not mean that the Pinots made from BV's Rutherford vineyards were bad, just not perfect. Nonetheless, when Knowles learned about the article, he met with André and berated him for his interview comments. Steinhauer recalled witnessing a "big fight" between Legh and André one day, in which Tchelistcheff became volatile and "very angry." Stuart Watson soon entered the fray as well. Fearing fallout for the BV brand, Watson announced that any future press interviews involving winery personnel would require the presence of a Heublein representative. André finally decided to severe his ties to Beaulieu: "Corporations are entirely different than private companies, and I started to gradually think we are not going to be successful in resisting any temptation, in jeopardizing this quality. It's time for me to go out." For the third time in his career at Beaulieu, André retired, this time on April 1, 1973. For André, however, retirement quickly transitioned into a lengthy and extraordinarily impactful consulting career.[32]

CHAPTER 7

The Consultant

André was an egalitarian.

—JILL DAVIS

On April 2, 1973, André left home at daybreak dressed in a spotless white short-sleeved shirt and neatly pressed light-blue trousers. When he returned to Napa that night, André walked through the front door of his Stonecrest Drive residence stained with wine from head to foot. "I found myself another home," André told Dorothy, "just like BV was when I went there in 1938!" The day after his retirement, André began consulting for Simi Winery in Sonoma County. Tchelistcheff's consulting career actually started in his earliest days in California, but this experience seemed different to him. André now felt "liberated" to choose a second career path as a consultant or, as he described it, a new "cycle of pioneering." André selected Simi for several reasons. First, Simi was historic, one of the oldest wineries in Sonoma County. Italian immigrants Giuseppe and Pietro Simi founded the winery in San Francisco in 1876 and moved it to Healdsburg, California, in 1881. Giuseppe's family became neighbors of the de Latours when newlyweds Georges and Fernande took up temporary residence in Healdsburg. In 1904 both Simi brothers died a month apart during an influenza outbreak, and the winery passed to Giuseppe's daughter Isabelle. During Prohibition, Isabelle Simi Haigh kept the winery operational by selling most of its vineyards and by cellaring its wines, and after the repeal, she opened the winery's first tasting room. André knew about Simi's heritage and, after World War II, even facilitated for Isabelle the construction of a small enological laboratory built by André's younger brother Victor. Despite André's assistance, Isabelle's winery fell into disrepair over the years, and in 1969 she decided to retire from the wine business. Isabelle sold her winery to Russell (Russ) Green, an oil executive from Los Angeles, who moved his family to Healdsburg in 1971 and began the expensive process of modernizing the facility. Thus, André identified an additional reason to consult for Simi: similar to Beaulieu in 1938, he discovered a rundown winery that might benefit from his expertise. Finally, and perhaps most important, André selected Simi because it was a family business. "I had been working for so many years for a family," André observed, "so I thought Mr. Green, and the family Green . . . would be the proper place for me to build a second professional home."[1]

When André launched his second career, he also believed that his thirty-five years in the wine industry, combined with his international connections, made it imperative for him to build a new generation of winemakers, just as, in his words, "I built already one." For Simi, he turned to a thirty-one-year-old novice winemaker named MaryAnn Graf, the first woman to graduate from the UC-Davis Fermentation Science program. After obtaining her undergraduate degree in 1965, her first jobs out of Davis were at commercial wine operations in California's Central Valley, where she grew up. André knew Graf from her attendance at various wine symposia and refresher courses at Davis, and he detected "a great sensibility of palate" in MaryAnn. Based on André's recommendation, Russ Green invited Graf for an interview for the head winemaker position at Simi in early April 1973. She met with Russ and André, and proceeded to engage in a five-hour "working interview." MaryAnn found it to be a "tremendous learning experience" but did not think she would get the job since she lacked winemaking experience with fine varietals. But André wanted her, so Russ hired MaryAnn on the spot.[2]

André drove to Healdsburg three days a week to work with Mary-Ann and Simi's cellar master Rick Sayre. "With André, you didn't just get an older, experienced winemaker who'd been doing it the same way for years and years and years," MaryAnn said. "You got a man who took in most recent information and had opinions about it" but who was also not afraid to change his mind. During the crush and fermentation process, André, then seventy-two, climbed to the top of the twenty-foot redwood tanks with Graf, leaped from tank to tank, and made observations about the frequency of pump overs and the importance of temperature control. André also took Graf into the vineyards to sample grapes and examine the vines. "André had a love of viticulture," MaryAnn said. "I think he saw very, very, very early on that the vineyard was probably one of the most important aspects [of winemaking]." Graf never felt threatened by André but still "jumped" when he said, "You must do this." When André was away for a few days, Graf and Sayre always "wanted to make sure we had all of our ducks lined up," MaryAnn recalled. "We never quite had everything sort of together," she said, but André never became angry. Instead, he always provided positive feedback, telling them, "Well that's great, but what about doing this?" All the while, Graf "was learning to be a winemaker, essentially." André continued to consult with MaryAnn at Simi over the next six years.[3]

When André selected MaryAnn Graf as Simi's winemaker, he played a significant role in bridging the gender gap in the California wine industry. Graf became the first woman winemaker of the modern era in California and eventually served as the first woman on the board of directors of the American Society for Enology and Viticulture. Other female winemaking students followed, including Jill Davis and Anne Moller-Racke at Buena Vista, Cheryl Barber Jones and Kay Simon at Chateau Ste. Michelle in Washington State, and Alison Green Doran at Firestone Vineyard in the Santa Ynez Valley. Alison, the daughter of Russ Green, worked as a harvest intern at Simi for six months in 1973, an experience that convinced her to switch majors from animal science to fermentation science at UC-Davis. Over the next three years, André assisted her in landing jobs in Alsace, France; in Paso Robles; and at Firestone. Alison began her career at Firestone as a lab technician, gradually worked her way up to the cellar master, and in 1981 took over as the head winemaker. She held that position for twenty-five years, the first twelve of which she worked closely with Firestone's consultant, André Tchelistcheff.

André's relationship with Firestone began in 1973. The previous year Leonard Firestone, heir to the Firestone Tire and Rubber Company fortune, purchased a 150-acre family ranch in Santa Barbara County's Santa Ynez Valley. One year later his son and daughter-in-law, Brooks and Kate Firestone, decided to transform the ranch into the county's first estate winery. At the suggestion of UC-Davis enology professor Albert Winkler, Brooks reached out to André with a consulting offer. At first André seemed reluctant; he did not know the region and feared that the project might result in a complete flop. Brooks told André, "Mr. Tchelistcheff, for years and years I have been selling something that stinks and that everybody hates to buy.... So I think [a pleasurable] bottle of wine will be nothing for me to sell." André agreed to consult, in part because of Firestone's willingness to assume a financial risk. Tchelistcheff, an aficionado of ballet and musical theater, also signed on to Firestone because Brooks's wife had previously danced as a prima ballerina in the Royal Ballet of London.[4]

After Alison Green took over as the head winemaker at Firestone, she met with André once a month during harvest season. Routinely, André and Alison tasted wine from early morning until midday, lunched at a Danish café in Solvang, and then spent three or four hours in the vineyards during the afternoon. André, whom she characterized as a "kind, gentle person," also insisted that Alison "keep notes on everything"—bud break, bloom, shoot growth, grape samples—eventually resulting in over two decades' worth of extensive vineyard data at Firestone. André taught her, first, that being a great winemaker required doing "above and beyond what you would normally do" and, second, to not waste his "time if you are unwilling to approach winemaking with a total effort." Alison felt that he wanted her to become recognized as an accomplished winemaker, not simply an accomplished "woman" winemaker. Alison also recalled that he always checked in with Firestone's cellar workers, whom he knew on a first-name basis. To André, "the people who made the wine were as important as the people who owned the winery," Alison said. She resided in a ranch house near the winery and raised horses, goats, and chickens. She recalled a dinner conversation one night during which André observed that one of her chickens appeared to have sour crop, a digestive disorder. He recommended feeding the chicken cream of wheat, followed several days later by pieces of melon. Alison heeded André's dietary advice and kept the chicken in her guest bathtub for two weeks until it fully recovered. At the time, Alison did not realize that André had published a book on poultry production in the 1930s.[5]

André's contributions to gender equality in the wine industry continued at Buena Vista. Jill Davis, Buena Vista's head winemaker between 1983 and 1994, called Tchelistcheff an egalitarian. "He saw us as winemakers, as students, not as male or female students," Jill said. She had become interested in winemaking in high school, when she accompanied her father to harvest Zinfandel grapes. She started dabbling in making wine and decided to enroll in UC-Davis's enology program in 1974. Davis graduated in 1978 with a bachelor of science degree in fermentation science after interning at Bear Mountain Winery in Bakersfield. Jill began her career at Beringer Vineyards working as an assistant to winemaker Myron Nightingale; then she transferred to Buena Vista in December 1982 as an assistant winemaker. Three months later, Jill, at twenty-seven years old, became its head winemaker when the previous winemaker unexpectedly resigned. "I didn't know where to start," Jill said. She then met Buena Vista's consultant, André Tchelistcheff, who mentored Davis through her next twelve vintages.[6]

Jill said that André had a gentle manner of teaching, patiently educating her on the nuances and fundamental skills of professional winemaking. He told her to start by tasting all of the wines and to pay attention to what the wine was telling her. "André taught me that if a wine needs something, do it now, not tomorrow," Jill said. André always tasted every one of the wines with her. If an issue arose, they would discuss the problem, and she felt compelled to resolve it by the time André returned for his weekly consulting visit. Jill observed that "the habits you learn from working with someone who could identify everything he tasted was incredible." André also taught Davis how to be a good manager, to care for her workers, and to recognize the importance of both disciplining *and* standing up for them. Essentially, "André taught me about life," Jill recalled. "Look at the winemakers who worked for him—they are all laser-focused people making great wine. I think he turned something on in us."[7]

Jill became one of André's favorite students, as did Rob Davis, a friend of hers, though not related. Rob grew up in Sacramento and attended UC-Davis as a premed major. His roommate studied enology, which required as much chemistry as the premed curriculum but seemed less intense. Rob decided to take a few wine classes and discovered a student cohort that was much more fun and far less cutthroat than his premed classmates. As a result, Davis switched majors, interned at Jordan Winery in Sonoma County's Alexander Valley, and graduated from UC-Davis with an enology degree in 1976. At the age of twenty-two, Rob was hired as the first head winemaker at Jordan Winery and met Jordan's new consultant, André Tchelistcheff. "I had no intention of spending the rest of my career at Jordan Winery," Rob said, "but that changed when I met André."[8]

André became Jordan's consultant in 1974. Two years earlier, Thomas Jordan, an oil executive from Denver, and his wife, Sally, purchased 275 acres of vineyards in the Alexander Valley. The Jordans were good friends with Baron Elie de Rothschild (who managed Bordeaux's historic Château Lafite-Rothschild), and Thomas served on the board of directors of the Banque Nationale de Paris. As Francophiles, the Jordans aspired to produce a California Cabernet Sauvignon on par with Bordeaux's first growths. The Jordans spent lavishly on their project—André estimated over $50 million—that included a magnificent, bright-yellow Habsburg-style château. Going for the best, they also reached out to André to consult for them. He accepted their offer, although he remained skeptical about the suitability of their property for Cabernet planting. He also insisted that the Jordans hire Rob Davis as their winemaker. Davis, André said, possessed "a tremendous head and technical knowledge, and a tremendous humanity in himself."[9]

At UC-Davis, Rob learned a great deal about how wine functions. What he did not learn, however, was how to manage crews, how to develop a working plan when the grapes come in, how to work with the grapes out in the vineyard, or even how to wash wine barrels properly. Davis bonded with André immediately because Tchelistcheff provided a wealth of expertise and a cosmopolitan perspective on how to make wine. Of all the insights André shared with Rob, the importance of terroir, especially the soil type, stood out as fundamentally important in the production of great wines. For example, as the Jordan family purchased the winery with the intention of producing Cabernets on par with Bordeaux's first growths, soon after Rob started his position, he took André to various vineyard locations to determine the best sites for Cabernet. Rob recalled one vineyard in particular that he thought would be perfect for Cabernet Sauvignon. "No, not Cabernet," André said. Rob then asked him if Merlot might be more suitable for the site. "No, not Merlot," André replied. "Well, André, what should we plant?" Rob inquired. "Alfalfa," André said. "Plant alfalfa." In keeping with André's advice, the Jordans planted 70 percent of that vineyard to hay and eventually sold it to the Lytton Rancheria in 2012.[10]

André called Rob "Doctor," based on Davis's successful research efforts in isolating malolactic bacteria, and invited him to join the Tchelistcheffs on a trip to France in 1978. "I thought he was a wine god here, but when I traveled to France with him everybody treated André with so much respect," Rob observed. During the trip, Rob also marveled at André's curiosity "for not just wine but for life" and at his remarkable stamina and endurance. "I was doing marathons at the time and I could not keep up with him," Davis said. Rob recalled an evening spent tasting wines in a cave in Châteauneuf-du-Pape, located in France's southern Rhône region. Well past midnight, Rob fell asleep and heard a loud clap. "Doctor, what's wrong with you?" André shouted. The French winemaker kept bringing up vintage after vintage and eventually ended the tasting with his finest cognac. André sipped the cognac, pounded his chest, and exclaimed, "Life! Cognac gives you life!" After turning in for a very short night—their next morning's first tasting appointment required a wake-up call at six o'clock—Rob lumbered out of bed, took a cold shower, and staggered to the hotel breakfast nook, longing for strong, black coffee. He wanted desperately to arrive at breakfast before André and was determined, as he put it, not "to let this old man show me up." Davis entered the room and encountered André and Dorothy sitting at their table, dressed impeccably, breakfasting together. "Well, Dorothy," André said, "I didn't think the Doctor would make it this morning."[11]

Regardless of André's needling, Rob regarded André as a father figure as well as a winemaking master. "There is something that has bound all of André's mentees," Rob said, "and that is our approach to wine." André taught his charges not to approach their task as producing "a stand-alone wine, revered for its singularity." What Rob called "André wines" stood out for their balance, beautiful acidity, and excellent fruit. André created wines for the table, "creating a memory, a memory to be shared with friends," Rob said. For André, "it was always about the finish—the round and soft finish and the memory of wine." To Rob, André represented something more than just an enologist and viticulturist. "André was also a poet," Rob said. "The poetry that defines his wines are the deeper part of André, exposing his soul to us." André often characterized wine in nontechnical terms, instead using romantic, even sensual imagery to capture the essence of a beautiful wine. To André, a great Pinot Noir displayed "the aroma of a dying black rose." He characterized an excellent Chardonnay as

smelling "like the breast of a young woman in winter wrapped in fur."
Rob believed that André's Chardonnay analogy arose directly from
Dr. Zhivago, Tchelistcheff's favorite movie. Early in the film, Tonya
Gromeko (played by Geraldine Chaplin) arrives in Moscow by train
from Paris and is greeted by Yuri Zhivago (played by Omar Sharif).
Beautiful Tonya, wrapped in fur, embraces Yuri on the train platform
in a poignant and intensely romantic scene.[12]

On various occasions, André related the musings of an old French
winemaker he had previously met in the Villages region of Beaujolais who compared the quality of a Grand Cru Burgundy, a Gamay
Beaujolais, and a Vin Rouge Ordinaire by referring to them as three
"ladies." The first lady who entered the tasting room wore an elegant,
black velvet dress. "Look at her hair," he said, "classically coiffed in the
back." She wore no makeup but possessed vital, deeply set eyes and lips
gently touched by beautiful pink. Her balanced torso and wonderfully
geometrical legs made a lasting impression. "She is the greatest red
Burgundy of the Côte d'Or," he said. Right outside the window the
second lady is singing a beautiful song. She wears a sheer blouse, and
as the wind passes, one sees the vibration of her breasts. Her cheeks
are pink. She is barefoot, beautiful, and excited to be alive. "She is a
Gamay Beaujolais," he said. The third lady walks by, and "God what a
crazy smell," a "killing, penetrating, crazy perfume." "Look at her hair,
look at her eyes, look at her cheeks," he said. "There is black, there is
purple, there is green, there is blue, and her lips are bloody red," he
observed. "Look at the way she moves her lips and her hips." One finds
it both upsetting and exciting. "Now, who is she?" he asked. Of course,
she is the "Vin Rouge Ordinaire de France."[13]

Rob observed that André's sensual metaphors were not meant to
offend. Instead, André believed that beauty in a wine represented its
core essence. He described wine as an "artistic pleasure of life" and compared wine to "folklore music." One must also remember, Rob said, that
André may have kissed women's hands or cheeks, an act that he meant
as a courtly gesture, but he always remained humble in the presence

of everyone. "André would literally kick you in the butt if you got too full of yourself," Rob said. "André provided a balance not just in wines but in his approach to life." He "taught us a humility about our work," Rob observed. In addition, despite all of the hardship André endured earlier in his life, he typically focused on the positive. "That positive approach is instilled in all of his students," Rob observed. On the one hand, he remembered complaining to André on one occasion about all of the problems he was encountering. "Doctor, behind every cloud there is a rainbow," André said. On the other hand, Rob also recalled once boasting about all of his good luck during a particular harvest season. André told him, "Doctor, there is always rain in the forecast." Rob eventually understood André's strategy as keeping him balanced, and he thanked his mentor for it. "We've been working together for four years. It has taken you that long to figure this out?" André asked.[14]

As a mentor, André always gave his students the freedom to make their own mistakes. "Even if he knew it was not the right thing to do, he knew you needed to *learn* from it," Rob said. He recalled an instance when he told André about trying something new on Cabernet fermentation. André told him, "Yes, yes, you should try it." When Rob's experiment failed, André told him, "I tried this back in 1948 and it made terrible wine." When André sampled the Cabernet, he told Rob that he would not even wash his shoes with it. "You learned that this is the type of structure you want to avoid," André told his pupil. "Wine is a very complex product," Rob observed. "We are taught about all of the things that can possibly go wrong, rather than what can go right. André helped me balance that out."[15]

Rob recalled that André loved being with his latest generation of students. Dorothy once said that André "thought young," embraced change, and always seemed extraordinarily spirited and youthful for his age. On one particular Christmas, Rob, dressed in a Santa Claus outfit, along with Jill Davis, Rick Sayre, and Chris Markell, showed up at the Tchelistcheff residence with a turkey, the trimmings, and a decked-out tree. All of a sudden André disappeared into the bedroom, leaving Rob somewhat puzzled. Dorothy said, "Don't worry, he has to be André. He has to be dressed appropriately." André soon reappeared in a coat and tie, and playfully leaped into Rob's lap. Since the occasion seemed so special, Rob composed a poem to commemorate it titled "A Christmas to Remember:"

'Twas the month before Christmas and all through the winery
Not a yeast was stirring, only Sach. Fermentati.
The tanks were all nestled in mold and fruit flies.
The winemaker was relaxing from the crush with a sigh.
The Chardonnay was sweet, showing no activity.
The Cabernet on the lees, what a calamity!

When up from the hill, who should appear?
But a man in a sports car with paraquat behind the ears.
The driver arose from his 240Z
Adorning a smile, seeming quite at ease.
His features were distinguished, from the country of the Czar,
His French shoes amuck with "gout de terroir."
He greeted us all, his eyebrows unfurled,
"Good Morning to you, Sir!", and kisses to the girls.

His stroll was quick as he went to work,
his smile to a frown, he began to jerk!
He glared at the winemaker, and said in a huff,
"There's problems here, Man, get off your butt!
Your stuck Chardonnay needs some yeast,
Ammonium phosphate, or vitamin B at least.
The Cabernet on the lees is getting reductive.
At this rate it will never finish the malolactic!
Start racking the tanks, and warm them up.
Top those tanks, and SO_2 adjust.
Bentonite, gelatin, we need to prepare.
Save the casein for my coffee," he said in despair.

The crew went to work and did just what he said.
Dreams of sugarplums were not in their heads!
His arms were folded, his worries were eased.
"Now I can smoke my Carltons in peace!"

The clock struck twelve, at home he must go
To plant bulbs in his garden with someone we all know.
(The Consultant Grand Cru has his own, you see;
He owes his guidance to his wife Dorothy.)
So the winery crew grouped for his departure to say,
"Merry Christmas to you, Dorothy, and to the man we call Andre!"[16]

Rick Sayre and Chris Markell, who joined Rob Davis in the Tchelistcheff Christmas celebration, remembered André as a legendary teacher and mentor. Both Sayre and Markell began working with André at Simi in the 1970s. In 1979 Sayre took over as the head winemaker at Rodney Strong Vineyards in Sonoma County and held the position for forty years. Markell, a viticulturist by training at UC-Davis, worked and consulted for wineries in California, France, Australia, Chile, and Hawaii. Both men noted André's passion for his craft, attention to detail, and obsession for sanitation. Each also took to heart his directive "must be done," instilling in them a sense of urgency when any problems surfaced. André also taught them about patience and perseverance. According to Chris, André once said, "If you want to be in this business, you need to be patient," advice that Markell always passed on to young winemakers. Sayre reflected that when he felt overwhelmed or depressed over a wine critic's negative feedback, he always recalled André's admonition, "You need to get a thick skin." Both also noted Tchelistcheff's willingness to learn, and they still marveled at his sensibility and expertise. Rick observed that André lacked the technical advances of the twenty-first century but still made great wines because "he always left it to Mother Nature to dictate what the vintage was going to be like." Chris said, "It was his depth of knowledge about everything. He knew more than we will ever know in our lifetimes."[17]

In 1978 Sayre, along with several other young winemakers, participated in one of André's wine tours to France. Rick recalled that everywhere the group went, the French winemakers "would roll out the red carpet." Rick also marveled at André's stamina. Each day the group arose early to visit at least six wineries and often did not eat dinner until 9 or 10 p.m. When visiting the Loire region, the group dined on copious amounts of salmon, asparagus, and Dijon mustard sauce every day. Rick appreciated the local fare and gracious hospitality, but by the end of the week, he had developed a craving for cheeseburgers. He also recalled tasting wine with Rob Davis and André in one of Loire's limestone caves. The owner, a local *négociant* (merchant), told them that he typically purchased wine from small producers, blended the wine, and bottled it, but he recently decided to experiment with making a barrel of his own. The négociant seemed very proud of his achievement but sought affirmation from the three winemakers. The wine, probably a Cabernet Franc, exhibited a pretty color, but its smell and taste revealed a cheesy, oxidized disaster. Not knowing what to say, André finally broke the silence. "Let me tell you," André said, "by its ruby color this has the look of a truly magnificent wine." After the three exited the cave and bid adieu to the owner, Rick and Rob took André aside and told him, "You always tell us to be forthright, never compromise, but you just praised an obviously flawed wine." André replied, "The wine looked like it needed a friend."[18]

Among all of the students André mentored, he took special pride in those who lacked any formal winemaking training but went on to become gifted winemakers. Three stood out: Lee Stewart at Souverain Cellars, Theo Rosenbrand at Beaulieu, and Michael Hoffman at Hoffman Mountain Ranch in Paso Robles, California. Dr. Stanley Hoffman, a cardiologist from Los Angeles, purchased the Paso Robles ranch property in 1961 and planted the first Pinot Noir vineyard in California's Central Coast. Assisted by his older son, David, a trained viticulturist, Hoffman at first produced a handful of barrels and sold the rest of his grapes to Mirassou Winery in the Santa Clara Valley. In 1973 Stanley and his wife, Terry, decided to expand production and sell their own wines. They reached out to André to gauge his interest in consulting for them. Intrigued, André and Dorothy made the road trip to the Central Coast. When they arrived at the ranch, the two discovered a beautiful property over seventeen hundred feet above Paso Robles and surrounded by almond and walnut groves. André met with Stanley and counseled caution in making such a substantial investment in an unknown region, but he also agreed to inspect the vineyards and offer an assessment. He went out to the vineyards and discovered "a beautiful situation, with the lime gravel, similar to Champagne and Burgundy," and observed the temperatures were moderated by the elevation and Pacific Ocean breezes. André agreed to consult.[19]

At first, André worked with David Hoffman, assisting him in pruning standards and in setting a vineyard regime. Meanwhile, Stanley's younger son, Michael, a bit of a troublemaking free spirit, was finishing his studies at California Polytechnic (or Cal Poly) in San Luis Obispo. When Michael returned home, André took this young man "with long hair" under his wing, determined to teach him the skills of winemaking. André believed that he possessed the intellect, artistic sense, and "tremendous boiling character" to succeed and encouraged the young Hoffman to quit drinking beer because it threatened to "carbonate his palate." Michael began meeting with André once a month and carefully followed Tchelistcheff's direction. He recalled calling André every night during the harvest and crush, and grew so fond of the man that he began calling him "Uncle André." Michael also remembered that when André arrived to consult, he always stopped by Terry's chicken coop to check on the chickens before going into the vineyards. Michael worked with André for the next fourteen years. During that period, André gave away Michael's wife at the Hoffmans' wedding, and the couple named their eldest daughter after André, Jennifer Andra Hoffman. "He was the best human ever," Michael reckoned.[20]

Even before André began consulting for Simi, Firestone, Jordan, and Hoffman Mountain Ranch, he decided to put his "energy into a region with entirely different dreams and goals of the achievements" that he had not been "able to achieve within the California ecological conditions." On the recommendation of his friend and noted wine writer Leon Adams, André chose Washington State. When Adams visited Washington's Yakima Valley in 1966, he saw several vineyards of Cabernet and Pinot Noir, and was astonished to discover that Washington's wineries typically blended their *vinifera* grapes with Concord. The result, in Adams's words, was "nondescript port and burgundy blends." The only fine wine Adams tasted, a Grenache rosé, came from a small winery called Associated Vintners, essentially a tiny collection of home winemakers who taught at the University of Washington. Adams then met with Victor Allison, manager of the state's only established winery at the time, American Wine Growers (AWG). He told Allison that excellent *vinifera* wines might be possible to produce but required the expertise of an outside consultant to get properly started. Adams recommended André Tchelistcheff. Allison contacted André and convinced him to travel to Seattle and sample AWG's table wines. André "wasn't too impressed," Dorothy said. During that trip, however, he tasted a Gewurztraminer produced by a home winemaker affiliated with Associated Vintners that Tchelistcheff regarded as stunning. He saw the potential and decided to put his energy into helping transform Washington's wine industry. He signed on as a consultant with AWG in 1967 and began making regular trips to Washington over the next two decades.[21]

André provided advice on pruning techniques, vineyard site selection, and grape varietals. He recommended that AWG concentrate on the white varietals Chardonnay, Gewurztraminer, and White Riesling, and Cabernet Sauvignon and Grenache for its reds. In 1969 AWG released its first *vinifera*-based wines under the label Ste. Michelle Vineyards, allegedly named after Mont-Saint-Michel off the Normandy coast. In the same year, the state of California sued Washington over the embargo it had placed on California wines under legislation passed in 1935. During legislative hearings, Dr. Walter Clore, a Washington State University horticulturist, testified in favor of changing the law to establish a more level playing field for California's wines. Clore argued convincingly that *vinifera* grapes could flourish in Washington, which is located in the same latitude as the premier wine-growing regions of France and possesses a longer growing season. Washington's state senators agreed and passed the 1969 California Wine Bill, effectively doubling the tax on its state's wines. The sudden overturning of the state's protectionist laws compelled AWG, and any new Washington winery, to immediately "up its game."[22]

In 1972 Wallace (Wally) Opdycke, a thirty-two-year-old executive in Seattle's Safeco Insurance Company, assembled a group of investors and purchased AWG. After conversations with Walter Clore, Opdycke became convinced that "within ten or fifteen years, Washington could be second only to California in grape and wine production." The following year the investment group recast the winery as Ste. Michelle Vintners, became part of the U.S. Tobacco of Connecticut conglomerate, and began to expand its acreage and production. In 1976 Ste. Michelle opened an impressive new winery facility in Woodinville, Washington, and renamed itself Chateau Ste. Michelle. With fewer than a dozen wineries in the state of Washington in the 1970s, Chateau Ste. Michelle literally set the standard for wine quality in the state and served as a role model for many of its aspiring vintners. In 1983 Ste. Michelle established Columbia Crest Winery on the banks of the Columbia River, which eventually became one of the state's largest and most acclaimed wineries. In 2009 *Wine Spectator* magazine ranked Columbia Crest's 2005 Reserve Cabernet Sauvignon the number 1 wine in the world for 2009. Meanwhile, Ste. Michelle, named America's winery of the year by *Wine Enthusiast* magazine in 2004 and *Wine & Spirits* in 2015, grew into a consortium of wineries and partnerships that became known as Ste. Michelle Wine Estates. A key part of this transformation occurred in 1995, when Ste. Michelle acted on André's suggestion to

THE CONSULTANT

partner with the famous Italian winemaker Piero Antinori. Working in tandem, Ste. Michelle and the Antinori family established the Col Solare winery on Washington's Red Mountain. Twelve years later, Ste. Michelle Wine Estates joined with the Antinori family to purchase Stag's Leap Wine Cellars, one of Napa Valley's most highly regarded wineries. Beginning with its bold move to hire André Tchelistcheff in 1967, Chateau Ste. Michelle became the engine powering the growth of the Washington State wine industry, which skyrocketed to become the second-leading national wine producer next to California by the twenty-first century.[23]

Two of Washington State's pioneering women winemakers, Cheryl Barber Jones and Kay Simon, worked with André beginning in the 1970s. Jones graduated from Washington State University in 1976 with a degree in food science and aspired to land a job in the dairy industry. With limited dairying positions available in the mid-1970s, Cheryl turned to the wine industry and landed a job at Chateau Ste. Michelle as a lab technician. She advanced quickly, was promoted to Ste. Michelle's white winemaker, and eventually became the head winemaker. Simon studied enology at UC-Davis and graduated with a degree in fermentation science in 1976. She worked briefly for United Vintners in the San Joaquin Valley before joining Chateau St. Michelle as the red winemaker in 1977. Following their employment at Ste. Michelle, both Jones and Simon became highly sought-after consultants, and Kay and her husband, Clay Mackey, started their own winery in the Yakima Valley.

Cheryl remembered André as a quiet, charming man but also a taskmaster. When he arrived at Chateau Ste. Michelle on his quarterly visits, André insisted that they sample wine from every single tank, starting at 9 a.m.; taking a short lunch break; and working the rest of the afternoon. "It was exhausting," Cheryl said. "After tasting wine all day all you want is a beer." Kay described André as nurturing and charming, as well as "a bit of a ladies' man." Kay said that one always expected "André to kiss your hand or your cheek," although she interpreted it as an Old World cultural practice rather than a "predatory thing." In fact, she never even considered "that André would diminish [women's] capabilities."[24] Jones believed that André's most significant impact at Chateau Ste. Michelle was in bringing a wealth of technical expertise to Washington's fledgling wine industry at the time. "Practical winemaking was just starting in Washington" in the 1970s, she said. Simon admired Tchelistcheff's "overarching understanding of enology and winemaking," knowledge based on his years of winemaking experience, as well as his international perspective. "He shared a lot of his world experience with us, and encouraged us to travel," Kay said. She also marveled at André's extraordinary palate. He "would taste very young wines, especially the reds, and provide an accurate analysis," Simon observed. "It is very tough to do that with young wines." Jones recalled accompanying Tchelistcheff in the company's private jet to visit Ste. Michelle's Columbia Crest winery in Paterson, Washington. "We would go out on a vineyard tour, and André knew *a lot* about the vineyards too," Cheryl said. She also remembered some of André's poetic analogies for wine. In one instance, André told her that the wine he just tasted reminded him of "a skunk running through a field of mint."[25]

Doug Gore, another gifted winemaker at Chateau Ste. Michelle, worked with André as well. A native of San José, California, Gore studied food science at Cal Poly, San Luis Obispo, in the 1970s. He landed his first job at Beringer in 1978 and for the next four years assisted winemaker Myron Nightingale. In 1982 Gore moved to Washington to take a winemaking position at Chateau Ste. Michelle, and the following year he moved to Paterson to become the head winemaker at Columbia Crest. Under Gore's direction, Columbia Crest became one of the state's largest wine operations, distinguishing itself in 2009 by producing *Wine Spectator*'s top-ranked wine in the world. Eventually, Gore became the executive vice president of winemaking and vineyard operations at Ste. Michelle Wine Estates and in 2017 was elected into the Washington Wine Hall of Fame. Gore regarded

André as a giant in the industry. "He brought us the news of the day" because "he always knew what was going on internationally," Doug said. He found André to be a "gracious guy" and a teacher and leader "who commanded your respect." André had an air about him that "just made you want to please him." Gore also thought Tchelistcheff was always looking ahead, trying new things, and never afraid to change his mind. Gore recalled a discussion with him over a technical matter in which Tchelistcheff had reversed his opinion "one hundred and eighty degrees" since their previous conversation. "André, you said the opposite last time we met," Gore remembered telling him. André replied, "Doug, you must always keep an open mind."[26]

André's foray into Washington State continued in 1978 when one of his nephews, Alex Golitzin, opened a new commercial winery in Snohomish. Alex, the son of André's sister Alexandra and her husband, Peter Golitzin, grew up in the Bay Area and fondly remembered summer visits to his uncle André's home in St. Helena. He recalled hunting rabbits and learning about wine. In 1967 Alex and his wife, Jeannette, moved their family to western Washington and, with André's help, began producing one barrel of Cabernet Sauvignon each year between 1974 and 1977. Pleased with the results, Alex opened Quilceda Creek Winery in Snohomish in 1978. He said that André helped considerably with Quilceda Creek's first crush in 1979 and was always available by telephone for Alex's multitude of questions. "Uncle André was very progressive," Alex said—a trait that could be confusing since he might change his mind from one conversation to the next—"but still helped us a lot with the details." Sourcing its grapes from eastern Washington's Horse Heaven Hills and Red Mountain, Quilceda Creek's reputation for producing outstanding Cabernet Sauvignon began to take off. After Alex's son Paul took over as the president and director of winemaking in 1993, the winery started scoring consistent 100-point wines in Robert Parker's *Wine Advocate*, produced *Wine Spectator*'s second-ranked wine of the year in 2003, and received international acclaim as one of America's finest Cabernet producers.[27]

When André made his consulting visits to Washington, he and Dorothy drove the eight hundred miles between Napa and the Seattle area. While passing through Oregon's Willamette Valley, André also stopped to chat with several Oregonian winemaking pioneers, including Dick Erath, Ed King Jr., and David Lett. Eventually, Erath and King hired André to consult for them. André never formally consulted with Lett but met with him on several occasions in the late 1960s and was twice invited to sample Lett's Pinot Noir and Chardonnay. The wines impressed Tchelistcheff, but he warned David not to "be too pleased" with his wines since he still had "a long ways to go." Nonetheless, André admired Lett's vision and work ethic, as well as the Willamette Valley's considerable potential for producing outstanding Pinot Noir. Lett, a graduate of UC-Davis's enology and viticulture program, established Eyrie Vineyards on the south end of Oregon's Dundee Hills in 1966. Believing that the region's soils and climate matched those of Burgundy, Lett planted the first *vinifera* vineyard in the Willamette Valley. The experiment paid off. Eventually, David became known as Oregon's "Papa Pinot" for his pioneering efforts in helping to bring Oregon's wine industry into the international spotlight. By the twenty-first century, Oregon catapulted to the nation's fourth-largest wine producer behind California, Washington, and New York.[28]

André's only consultancy outside of the United States took place in Bolgheri, Italy, located in the heart of Tuscany's coastal region, Maremma. While attending Vinexpo in Bordeaux in 1981, André was introduced to Piero Antinori's younger brother, Lodovico, by Tchelistcheff's friend Darrell Corti. A renowned wine and food expert, Corti worked for Corti Brothers, a family market in Sacramento noted for its collection of international wines and gourmet delicacies from around the world. From the beginning of his career at Corti Brothers, Darrell traveled internationally in search of gastronomical gems that his family store could introduce to America. On one of these trips, he visited Bolgheri and was invited to meet with Lodovico Antinori at his newly inherited estate, Ornellaia. Lodovico wanted to start a

winery that could produce wines rivaling the Bordeaux-style Super
Tuscans of his uncle, Mario Incisa della Rocchetta, and his brother,
Piero. Following Corti's advice, Lodovico hired André to consult for
him. Lodovico had once considered buying vineyards in California,
but when André assessed the clay soils and the cool maritime climate
of Maremma, he told Antinori, "Forget about California, this is El
Dorado." Instead of planting Cabernet Sauvignon, Lodovico's original
preference, he accepted the advice of Tchelistcheff as well as Corti
and went with Merlot instead. Within two decades, the winery that
Antinori named Tenuta dell'Ornellaia produced *Wine Spectator*'s top-
ranking wine of the year.[29]

André's consultancies continued to accumulate until February 1991,
when Heublein enticed him to return to Beaulieu Vineyard as its
consulting enologist. "When I walked back into the winery there were
tears in the eyes of the older employees who remembered me," André
said, "and it gave me great spiritual satisfaction and pleasure." During
the previous eighteen years, his contracts had taken him far and wide.
In Napa Valley alone, the sites included Clos Pegase Winery, Conn
Creek Winery, Franciscan Estate, Niebaum-Coppola Estate Winery,
Sequoia Grove Winery, Stag's Leap Wine Cellars, Swanson Vineyards,
and Villa Mt. Eden Winery. Characteristically, André put his heart
and soul into consulting, offering hands-on advice and follow-up far
beyond his contractual obligations, and he often charged no fees at all.
In the mid-1960s, for example, André offered free advice to Jack and
Jamie Davies, assisting them in gearing up for their first crush at Napa
Valley's Schramsberg Vineyard, which they had recently purchased
and restored. A crowd that included André and a reporter from the *St.
Helena Star* gathered for the big event. To the Davies' dismay, however,
the crusher failed to start. André turned to Jamie and said, "My dear,
your duty is clear. Load the press from the boxes and get in there and
stomp the grapes." Joined by the vineyard foreman's daughter, Jamie
took off her shoes, climbed into the winepress, and proceeded to stomp,
forever endearing the Davies to André and he to them. André later

reflected that the Davies family became his "nearest, closest friends in the Napa Valley."[30]

During André's second career as a freelance consultant, he never seemed to slow down. Accompanied by Dorothy, he continued to travel, attend White House dinners, lecture, and mentor, and he routinely climbed ladders to the top of storage tanks to sample wine even into his early nineties. For relaxation, André loved to fish. When he worked at Beaulieu, André used to fly fish in the local creeks with Joe Heitz, although Heitz could not recall ever actually catching any fish. André and Dorothy also made a number of salmon fishing trips out of San Francisco, guided by Leon Adams in his versatile angling craft. In addition, for several years Ste. Michelle sponsored annual fishing excursions to the Caribbean, transporting the Tchelistcheffs to Belize's largest island, Ambergris Caye. Dorothy fondly recalled watching the local fishing crews doing their best to assist André, especially when seagulls tried to snatch his bait.[31]

Between the time André left Beaulieu in 1973 and returned in 1991, Napa Valley underwent dramatic change. In 1981 its vintners and growers adopted the valley's own Appellation d'Origine Contrôlée system. The entire valley became the first American Viticultural Area (AVA) to be designated in California and only the second in the United States. Over the next three decades, sixteen additional nested AVAs followed: Los Carneros (1983), Howell Mountain (1983), Wild Horse Valley (1988), Stags Leap District (1989), Mt. Veeder (1990), Atlas Peak (1992), Spring Mountain District (1993), Oakville (1993), Rutherford (1993), St. Helena (1995), Chiles Valley (1999), Diamond Mountain District (2001), Oak Knoll District of Napa Valley (2004), Calistoga (2009), and Coombsville (2011). Even before the AVA system went into effect, André argued that Napa Valley should be divided into sixteen appellations. He envisioned each of these appellations within three subregions. André regarded the southern sector, between Los Carneros and Yountville, as Napa's equivalent of Burgundy. Here, varietals such as Chardonnay and Pinot Noir could thrive. The central sector, between Yountville and St. Helena, constituted Napa's Bordeaux region, according to Tchelistcheff. Cabernet Sauvignon, Merlot, and Malbec typically flourished in this microclimate. For the region running north of St. Helena to Calistoga, the northern sector, André favored Rhône varietals such as Syrah and Grenache but believed it could excel in Cabernet Sauvignons and Sauvignon Blancs as well. According to wine law and policy attorney Richard Mendelson, André believed that each appellation and subregion displayed "unique and viticulturally distinctive geographical features," making it imperative "that the quality of the wines made from the grapes be controlled both in the vineyard and in the winery."[32]

The 1970s and '80s also witnessed a burst of land and winery transactions that, in the words of wine historian Charles Sullivan, "placed ownership of Napa Valley in a constant state of flux." Grape production doubled, the number of wineries tripled, wine prices spiked, and the demand for Napa Valley wines increased dramatically. Yet despite becoming home to the country's first agricultural preserve in 1968, the valley also began to experience an upsurge in environmental battles over land use, water quality, and hillside development. In addition, tourists from all corners of the earth started pouring into the region, accompanied by starstruck millionaires hungering for a piece of the valley's valuable real estate. Anyone who remembered Napa Valley in the 1960s might not have recognized it by the early 1990s. The valley's pastoral simplicity, sleepy towns, and modest wineries gave way to luxury hotels and resorts, Michelin-starred restaurants, and scores of wineries featuring tours and tastings, picnic facilities, gift shops, and art exhibits. In the 1960s, the Northern Pacific Railroad ran on a single track parallel to Highway 29 and managed the shipping needs of the valley's wineries. By the early 1990s, the former railroad morphed into a "wine train," transporting *vin*-sipping tourists through the valley in the soothing comfort of air-conditioned carriages. Another significant change took place in 1981 when the Napa Valley Vintners introduced an annual wine auction that raised millions of dollars for local charities.

The auction also provided the setting, writes wine historian Thomas Pinney, in which "the very rich and fashionable [competed] with one another to astound the simple bourgeois by the extravagance of their ... astonishing bids and bacchanalian revelry."[33]

André began to worry about the money flowing into the valley, the excesses of material wealth, and the shift away from the core values that shaped Napa Valley's phenomenal success in the first place. He once said, "Money is the dust of life. I don't have a wine cellar, I don't have a vineyard. . . . I only have my head." In 1990 he told Margrit Biever Mondavi that he felt Napa Valley had gone a "bit too far with self-admiration" and had become a "bit too gaudy" and that "this gaudiness" had the possibility of losing a part of Napa Valley's "charming authority." In an interview the following year with the *Los Angeles Times* wine critic Dan Berger, André lamented these changes and said that "the tragedy of us today [is that] people are guided by big ideas, big dreams, big images, but nobody likes to do fundamental [work] in winemaking." André believed that too many winemakers "are not living with wines anymore, they are in offices." Tchelistcheff insisted that winemakers must be not only in touch with the wine but also in contact with every employee. "You have to talk with your staff," he said. "That includes the grower, the man in charge of crush, even the man in charge of barrel washing, every little thing."[34]

Despite his misgivings about the future, André continued to garner award after award, not only from the French government, the American Society of Enologists, *Wine Spectator*, and the Culinary Institute of America at Copia, but also from such entities as the James Beard Foundation, the American Wine Society, the Society of Bacchus, and the Comune di San Gimignano. The famous German artist and musician Wolfgang Alexander Kossuth even sculpted a bust of André during a sitting at Tuscany's Tenuta dell'Ornellaia. Yet along with the accolades and punishing schedule, André's health also began its steady decline. Shortly after he celebrated his ninety-second birthday in December 1993, doctors diagnosed Tchelistcheff with esophageal cancer. He had quit cigarettes in 1991, but years of heavy smoking had taken their toll. André started an arduous regimen of radiation treatments, yet even then he carried on with his vineyard and winery activities. However, in late March 1994, André underwent emergency surgery at Napa's Valley of the Queen Hospital to remove a stomach tumor. Combined with the spread of his cancer, the surgical trauma pushed André's frail constitution beyond its limit. "Until the last day his mind was fighting," Dorothy said. "When it became inevitable that he would lose, after receiving last rites from a Russian Orthodox priest, he told me: 'I am ready to go.'" Dorothy observed, "He was so peaceful." On Tuesday, April 5, 1994, André Viktorovich Tchelistcheff, who had cheated death on more than one occasion in the past, took his final breath.[35]

The following Monday, an overflow crowd of five hundred people gathered for André's memorial service at St. Mary's Episcopal Church in Napa. According to a reporter from the *Napa Valley Register* who covered the event, "There was more laughter than tears." Over the next hour and a half, André's friends and associates eulogized him as a wine master, teacher, poet, philosopher, and humanitarian. Speakers referred to André's romantic spirit and his disdain for material possessions, as well as his love of nature. Rob Davis, one of André's star pupils, spoke of his abiding affection for André, whom he regarded as a second father. Davis told stories about André's wine tours in France and his mentor's propensity for sleeping in the winery during the harvest to take note of the wine's "enological murmurs." Phil Hiaring, the publisher of *Wines & Vines* magazine, recalled Tchelistcheff's fondness for poetic metaphors, observing that "André was the only person in the world who could say a 'Chardonnay wine is like a beautiful woman's breast wrapped in fur' and get away with it." Legh Knowles, the longtime marketing director at Beaulieu, told the gathering of his mental search for the proper characterization of André Tchelistcheff. After much thought, the solution proved to be unsurprisingly simple: "*Maestro*," Knowles concluded, fittingly captured the man and his legacy.[36]

6. André as a consulting enologist. Courtesy of Dorothy Tchelistcheff.

7. André and Dorothy with the Reagans at a White House dinner on October 8, 1985. Courtesy of Dorothy Tchelistcheff.

8. Bronze statue of André sculpted by American artist William Behrends in the courtyard outside Beaulieu Vineyard's reserve tasting room in Rutherford. Photograph by author.

9. Clay bust of André sculpted by German artist Wolfgang Alexander Kossuth during a sitting at Tuscany's Tenuta dell'Ornellaia. Photograph by author.

10. André Tchelistcheff, the "winemaker's winemaker." Courtesy of Dorothy Tchelistcheff.

CHAPTER 8

The Tchelistcheff Tour, Part 2

Money is the dust of life. I don't have a wine cellar, I
don't have a vineyard. . . . I only have my head.

—ANDRÉ TCHELISTCHEFF

The day after its arrival in Paris in 1976, the Tchelistcheff group took
part in a hosted tasting of French wines at Chemin des Vignes, the
bottling and storage warehouse in Paris's factory district that Steven
Spurrier shared with Lucien Legrand. Following the tasting, the group
met with Pierre Bréjoux, the inspector general of France's Appellation
d'Origine Côntrolée Board, to discuss their three-week itinerary. Joanne
Dickenson DePuy said that Bréjoux "treated André like royalty." She
also observed that "André was much loved in Paris." The following day,
May 9, 1976, the group traveled to Montmartre in Paris's eighteenth
arrondissement. The historic district featured the white-domed Basil-
ica of the Sacré-Coeur and during the Belle Epoque attracted artists
such as Claude Monet, Pierre Auguste Renoir, Edgar Degas, Henri de
Toulouse-Lautrec, Pablo Picasso, and Vincent van Gogh. In addition,
at the corner of Rue Saint-Vincent and Rue des Saules was situated
Clos Montmartre, the city's only vineyard. Planted in 1933 by the city
to offset urban sprawl, Clos Montmartre also served as the place where
André completed his practical training during his student days in Paris.
Based on this experience, André later recalled, "I decided to specialize

in viticulture," which he said became "my first love, even over enology, though my successes in life [were] enological ones."[1]

On May 10, the Tchelistcheff tour proceeded east to Epernay, situated in the heart of the Champagne region. André landed his first winery job in France at Moët et Chandon, one of Epernay's most historic champagne houses. Founded in 1743 by Claude Moët during the reign of Louis XV (1715–74), Moët produced a sparkling wine that was in great demand at the time by the French royalty. In fact, champagne became the perfect accompaniment at Louis's court, one notorious for its "licentiousness and promiscuity, where food and sex held center stage." The marquise de Pompadour, Louis's official chief mistress from 1745 to 1751, once said that champagne was the only wine "that left a woman beautiful after drinking it." By the late eighteenth century, Moët's sparkling wine company expanded into the international market under Claude's grandson, Jean-Rémy Moët. During one of Jean-Rémy's promotional excursions in 1782, he met and befriended a young man named Napoleon Bonaparte at a military school in Brienne-le-Château. Enchanted by Moët's product and while serving as French emperor (1804–14), Napoleon later ordered caseloads of its champagne for his troops. As Bonaparte once said, "Champagne! In victory one deserves it, in defeat one needs it." When Jean-Rémy's son-in-law, Pierre-Gabriel Chandon de Briailles, joined the company as a partner in 1833, its name changed to Moët et Chandon. Sales of its label Brut Imperial soared over the next century. In 1921 Moët et Chandon introduced its famous luxury label Dom Pérignon, named after a seventeenth-century Benedictine monk and cellar master, and released it for sale in 1936.[2]

During the early stages of its occupation of France during World War II, the German Army requisitioned Moët et Chandon. Troops destroyed the Chandon château on the grounds of Dom Pérignon's abbey and took over most of the other winery buildings. The Germans also ordered the company to supply the Third Reich with fifty thousand bottles of champagne a week. In response, Moët's upper management actively supported the French Resistance by welcoming "the Resistance [operatives] into Moët's twenty-four kilometers of cellars." Eventually the Nazi Gestapo intervened and dispatched nearly every one of Moët's top managers to prisons or concentration camps. Despite its horrific ordeal during the war, afterward the company recovered quickly. In the 1950s, Moët et Chandon obtained an exclusive royal warrant to supply its product to Britain's Queen Elizabeth II, expanded into the Napa Valley (Domaine Chandon) in 1973, and merged with Hennessy Cognac and Louis Vuitton in the final decades of the twentieth century to become the largest champagne house in the world.[3]

Following the visit in Epernay, the Tchelistcheff group continued east to Arbois, where members met with the prominent French grower-négociant Henri Maire. Maire owned 90 percent of the vineyards in Arbois, including one that once belonged to Louis Pasteur. Located on the Franco-Swiss border in northern Burgundy, Arbois was the birthplace and boyhood home of Pasteur. Pasteur linked sugar's conversion to alcohol in grape juice, the process known as fermentation, to the living organisms called yeasts. In addition, he also discovered how bacteria spoil milk. He demonstrated that bacteria did not spontaneously generate but were instead introduced into the milk as a result of poor sanitation standards and exposure to air. Pasteur discovered that heating the liquid to near boiling could kill the foreign microbes, and the process became known as pasteurization. A boon to the dairy industry, Pasteur's discoveries aided winegrowers as well by showing them how to control the level of volatile acidity in wine that, if too high, can turn wine into vinegar. Wine scholars credit Pasteur's remarkable research as the catalyst for the modern field of enology, and he clearly provided the inspiration for André's fastidious approach to winery sanitation.[4]

After its stopover in Arbois, the Tchelistcheff tour proceeded southwest into the heart of Burgundy and visited "the single largest vineyard in Burgundy and one of the most famous in the world." The Grand Cru (Great Growth) vineyard Clos de Vougeot, established by Cistercian monks in the twelfth century, comprised 125 acres of vines planted primarily to Pinot Noir. At the outset of the French Revolution, Clos de Vougeot as well as most of the vineyards of the Côte d'Or region belonged to the church. During the revolutionary and Napoleonic era, however, the state seized the properties and distributed them to local peasants, who in turn parceled them out to their children. As a result, the great vineyards such as Clos de Vougeot continued to exist as an entity but as one eventually subdivided among eighty owners. Thus, separate wines coming from the same vineyard often displayed different characteristics depending on the age of the vines and the skill set of the grower. Nevertheless, the late wine expert Alexis Lichine regarded the Clos de Vougeot vineyard "so famous that it [was] practically a national monument in France," producing wines that ranked among the most treasured and costly in the world. Equally impressive, the château on the historic property featured a dining room that could seat five hundred people and exhibited old leather harvest baskets inscribed with the dates of noteworthy vintages, beginning with 1108.[5]

On nearly every day of the three-week journey, the Tchelistcheff group visited five or six wineries, and the French winemakers often treated the Americans to some of their appellation's best vintages. Andy Beckstoffer remembered that at Petrus, one of Bordeaux's most exclusive Right Bank châteaus, the French vintner "pulled out maybe nineteen years' worth of wine." André translated for the group at every stop, making practical use of his perfect Parisian French. Joanne Dickenson DePuy recalled the excitement of being the first group of California wine professionals to meet with their French counterparts, but she also clearly recollected everyone's sheer exhaustion. "We took voluminous notes, wined and dined," and "barely hit [our] beds before it all began again the next day," Joanne said. She remembered one instance of returning to the hotel around 9 p.m., where she met with some of its lobby staff to plan logistics for the next day. All of a sudden the elevator door opened and out walked André with Pierre Bréjoux and Dorothy. "They are trying to kill me!" André exclaimed. Despite his amusing plaint in this instance, Dickenson DePuy described André as "indefatigable," going strong at all hours and even "wearing out the young people on the tour."[6]

André "ran a tight ship," according to Joanne. He "didn't take much guff from anyone," Louis Martini said. Tchelistcheff insisted that the group be ready to board the bus by 8:30 a.m. every day. "André made sure we met every obligation and arrived at every event on time," Dickenson DePuy said. Beckstoffer remembered thinking "that some of these upstart Americans were going to venture into the inner sanctum of the wine world of Europe. And we were told, 'Don't ask too many questions. You're the new kids on the block. Don't be pushy Ugly Americans. Just be careful about what you do.'" Martini recalled one instance when André caught wind that some of the wives on the tour were starting to complain about the long days, the constant wine tasting, and the lack of shopping time. André got up in front of the bus and said, "I want you to know that this was billed as a winemaker's tour. Then we're going to visit wineries and vineyards and that's all laid out. Some of the young people in the group actually borrowed money to take this tour, and I'm going to see that they learn as much as they possibly can.'"And that was that," Louis said. In addition to his respect for André's decisive leadership, the way in which the French winemakers received Tchelistcheff also impressed Martini. "I mean, you'd think he was one of them," Louis observed.[7]

The Tchelistcheff tour completed its action-packed itinerary in Bordeaux, visiting Right Bank wineries in Pomerol and Saint-Emilion and Left Bank châteaus in Graves and Haut-Médoc. Bordeaux's system of vineyard ownership, where large estates fell under the control of one entity, contrasted sharply with that of Burgundy. While in Haut-Médoc, the Californians visited the historic Château Palmer. Named after the English military officer Charles Palmer who acquired the ancient estate in 1814, the third-growth winery was purchased by a syndicate in 1938 that included the Miailhe family. The Miailhes, among France's leading wine producers, also owned several châteaus:

Pichon Longueville, Siran, Coufran, Dauzac, and Citran. As noted previously, when the German Army occupied France during World War II, most of the country's best vineyards came under German control, including those in Bordeaux. Less than a week after their arrival in the Haut-Médoc, the Germans requisitioned the Miailhes' principal residence, Château Pichon Longueville-Comtesse de Lalande, and told the family to find another place to live. The Miailhes moved in with their grandparents, who lived at Château Siran in neighboring Margaux, and joined a throng of distant relatives who had fled to the estate from northern France. Two Italian Jewish families, friends of the Miailhes', temporarily inhabited Château Palmer. "We knew [our Italian friends] were no longer safe there," May-Elaine Miailhe de Lencquesaing said, "so we decided on a temporary measure and moved the two families into a small annex attached to the château." The Miaihles added a small trapdoor to supply their friends with food and messages. Days later, the Germans requisitioned Château Palmer.[8]

The Miailhes worried incessantly about the security of their Jewish friends. They watched in horror as the Germans set up a transit camp for Jews on the outskirts of Bordeaux and mandated that all of the city's Jews wear yellow Stars of David. What prompted the Miailhes to act on their friends' behalf, however, was an atrocity that took place in Paris the third week of July 1942. With the assistance of French police, the Germans launched their first roundup of Jews since the beginning of the Nazi occupation. Three thousand men, fifty-eight hundred women, and four thousand children were detained. The Germans held sixty-nine hundred of the detainees in the cycling arena Vélodrome d'Hiver for an entire week with little food or water before transferring them to internment camps. From there, the Germans then loaded their Jewish victims onto trains bound for Auschwitz. (Most never returned.) With the lives of the four adults and three children hidden in Palmer's secret annex now at stake, the Miailhe brothers Edouard and Louis devised an escape plan. For the past two years, the brothers had visited the Palmer estate's vineyards regularly, ostensibly to monitor the vines but also to smuggle food and supplies into the annex. On a clandestine night visit to the Palmer estate in the summer of 1942, the Miailhe brothers liberated their Italian friends and led them to safety. An ocean liner out of Bayonne then transported all seven Italians to Argentina. At every stage of their perilous escape, the Italians used forged identity documents the Miailhes had obtained from a retired French Canadian military officer named Raymond Brutinel. During the war, Brutinel operated an escape network for stranded British airmen out of his home, Château Lascombes.[9]

Château Lascombes, as it turned out, became the last stop for the 1976 Tchelistcheff tour. The Californians attended a farewell luncheon at the château, a second-growth winery in Margaux, situated in the Haut-Médoc region on the western side of the Gironde estuary. Alexis Lichine, who co-owned Lascombes from 1952 to 1971, hosted the event. Born in Moscow in 1913, Lichine and his family fled Russia at the outset of the Bolshevik Revolution. After a brief residence in New York City, the Lichine family moved to Paris, joining the sizable Russian exile community in the City of Light. In 1935 Lichine returned to New York to work in a wine retail shop, a position that led to a career in importing and writing about wine. After serving as a major in army intelligence in World War II, Lichine returned to the wine-importing business, divided his time between New York and Bordeaux, and founded Alexis Lichine & Company. In 1951 Lichine published his first in a series of books on wine, *The Wines of France*. After multiple editions, it was later republished as *Alexis Lichine's Guide to the Wines and Vineyards of France*, sealing his reputation as one of the world's leading experts on French wine.[10]

Lichine arranged for the Tchelistcheff group to meet with fifty Bordeaux vintners, and he organized a guided tour followed by apertifs and lunch. During the champagne apertif, a uniformed staffer approached Joanne and told her that someone called and was asking to speak with a Tchelistcheff participant named Monsieur (Jim) Barrett. Joanne could not understand how anyone—outside of Bréjoux, André, their travel agent in Paris, or herself—could know of the group's whereabouts, and she worried that the call might concern one of Barrett's children. The staff member accompanied Joanne and Jim to a small office, where Barrett took the call. The caller turned out to be George Taber, a *Time* magazine reporter who had covered the Steven Spurrier–Patricia Gastaud-Gallagher tasting event in Paris the previous day. Barrett, the owner of Napa Valley's Chateau Montelena Winery, identified himself, spoke briefly, and flashed Joanne the okay sign. "Have you heard that your wine came in first in the tasting that was held on Monday in Paris?" Taber asked. Barrett replied, "No, I haven't," but "that's great." Taber told him the Montelena's '73 Chardonnay, made by Mike Grgich, won in the white wine category and that Warren Winiarski's Stag's Leap '73 Cabernet Sauvignon captured the reds. Taber then asked, "What's your reaction to beating the French at their own game and in Paris?" After a brief pause, Barrett responded, "Not bad for kids from the sticks."[11]

The wine tasting in Paris took place at the Intercontinental Hotel on May 24, 1976. Steven Spurrier and Patricia Gastaud-Gallagher, who advertised the event as a bicentennial celebration honoring both the United States and France, decided that it should be a blind tasting in which the judging panel would not be able to see the wine labels. Spurrier selected twelve California wines—six Chardonnays and six Cabernet Sauvignons—to be tasted alongside four French white Burgundies and four red Bordeaux. In the white wine category, Spurrier chose a '74 Chalone Vineyard, a '73 David Bruce, a '72 Freemark Abbey, a '73 Spring Mountain, a '72 Veedercrest Vineyard, and a '73 Chateau Montelena. These wines were matched up with a '73 Bâtard-Montrachet Ramonet-Prudhon, a '73 Meursault Charmes Roulot, a '73 Beaune Clos des Mouches Joseph Droughin, and a '72 Puligny-Montrachet Les Pucelles Domaine Leflaive. The California Cabernets included a '72 Clos du Val, a '69 Freemark Abbey, a '71 Mayacamas, a '71 Ridge, a '70 Heitz, and a '73 Stag's Leap. Spurrier matched the Cabernets with Bordeaux classics that included a '70 Château Montrose, a '71 Château Léoville–Las Cases, a '70 Château Mouton Rothschild, and a '70 Château Haut-Brion.[12]

Spurrier consciously chose French wines that he thought its country's judges would find significantly superior to California's best. He also selected a tasting panel that included some of France's leading wine experts: Inspector General Pierre Bréjoux of the Appellation d'Origine Contrôlée Board; Michel Dovaz, a teacher at Spurrier's Académie du Vin; Claude Dubois-Millot, the sales director of *Gault & Millau*; Odette Kahn, the editor of France's leading wine review, *La Revue du vin de France*; Raymond Oliver, chef and owner of Le Grand Véfour restaurant, a perennial favorite over the years of notables such as Voltaire, Napoleon, and Jean-Paul Sartre; Pierre Tari, the secretary general of the Association des Grands Crus Classés; Christian Vannequé, head sommelier of La Tour d'Argent; Aubert de Villaine, the co-owner of the legendary winery Domaine de la Romanée-Conti; and Jean-Claude Vrinat, owner of the three-Michelin-star restaurant Taillevent.[13]

Shortly after 3 p.m. on the twenty-fourth, Spurrier addressed the nine panelists. He described the event as a celebration of America's bicentennial and France's important role in its war for independence, as well as an opportunity to compare several interesting wines coming out of California with some of France's best. Steven also told the judges that he and Patricia decided that a blind tasting helped ensure the highest standard of objectivity. He asked the tasting panel to evaluate each wine on the basis of four criteria—eye (color and clarity), nose (aroma), mouthfeel (taste and structure), and harmony (the combination of all the sensations)—and that each wine be scored on a twenty-point scale. George Taber, the only journalist in the room, witnessed the proceedings.[14]

Prior to the event, Gastaud-Gallagher gave Taber a list of the wines with the tasting order, so he could easily follow along and note the judges' reactions. Taber recalled nervous laughter and quick side comments from the panelists early on. Soon, however, he realized that the judges seemed completely confused with the white wines, experiencing considerable difficulty in differentiating between California Chardonnays and their French counterparts. For example, Raymond Oliver was absolutely convinced he had just tasted a French white, which instead happened to be a wine from Napa Valley's Freemark Abbey. Claude Dubois-Millot felt certain that he was tasting a California white wine "because it had no nose." Ironically, it turned out to be one of France's most iconic white Burgundies, Bâtard-Montrachet. Dubois-Millot later confessed to Taber that "we thought we were recognizing French wines, when they were California and vice versa. At times we'd say that a wine would be thin and therefore Californian, when it wasn't. Our confusion showed how good California wines have become."[15]

Before the reds were distributed for tasting, Spurrier announced the results in the white wine category. Napa Valley's '73 Chateau Montelena scored highest, followed by the '73 Meursault Charmes Roulot from Burgundy's famed Côte d'Or. California Chardonnays from Chalone, Spring Mountain, and Freemark Abbey placed third, fourth, and sixth, respectively. According to Taber, the judges' reactions "ranged from shock to horror." Every single panelist rated a California Chardonnay first, with the Chateau Montelena favored by six of the nine judges. Spurrier and Gastaud-Gallagher participated in the blind tasting as well and scored the California wines more critically. Steven's scorecard placed the Bâtard-Montrachet and Freemark Abbey in a tie for first. Patricia's analysis resulted in a tie for top ranking as well between Meursault Charmes and Spring Mountain. As the room buzzed, Taber "felt a sense of both awe and pride," as well as "some chauvinism that a California white wine had won."[16]

Given the stunning results and the palpable consternation among some of the judges, Spurrier figured that a California red did not stand a chance of winning the next tasting round. He believed that French reds, with their characteristic restraint, balance, and complexity, would be easier to distinguish from California's bolder, more fruit-forward Cabernets. To Taber, the French judges now seemed "more intense and circumspect" than before, with far less chatter in the room. At one point, Christian Vannequé exclaimed, "That's a California, or I don't know what I'm doing here." Taber glanced at his list and verified the accuracy of the sommelier from La Tour d'Argent; he had just tasted a Ridge Monte Bello. Raymond spotted a "Mouton, without a doubt," he said, a correct observation once again. The tasting ended at 6 p.m., far later than expected, so Spurrier quickly read the results. This time, French reds placed second, third, and fourth. In addition, compared to the white wine category, the French reds scored much higher than the California wines. However, the panel's top-ranked wine turned out to be the '73 Stag's Leap Wine Cellars Cabernet Sauvignon from Napa Valley. "The judges sat in disbelief," Taber observed. Even Odette Kahn, one of France's most astute wine critics, ranked Stag's Leap first. Immediately after Spurrier read the results, Kahn marched up to Steven and demanded that he turn over her scorecards. "I'm sorry, Madame Kahn," Spurrier said, "but you're not going to get them back." Spurrier then instructed his summer intern to gather all the scorecards and take them to the Académie du Vin straightaway for safekeeping.[17]

Shortly after he ended his phone conversation with George Taber, Jim Barrett took Joanne Dickenson DePuy aside in Lascombe's crowded dining room and whispered, "That was a reporter from *Time* magazine. Our white wine just won Steven's tasting, and Warren [Winiarski] won the reds." Not knowing what to do, Joanne approached André to solicit his advice. "Don't say a word," André said. "We must not let the French know of this." Joanne passed on André's guidance to Barrett, but word had already spread throughout the Tchelistcheff group. Despite this, no one uttered a word to their French hosts, even after Alexis Lichine's patronizing luncheon address in which he told the Americans about his faith in their capacity to produce some very good wines at some point in the future. In the late afternoon, the Californians bid adieu to their French hosts, boarded the bus, and waved goodbye as they rolled down the winery's driveway. According to Joanne, once the bus turned the corner, "the entire bus erupted." Andy Beckstoffer recalled Barrett's euphoric exclamation: "Hot damn! We knocked 'em in the creek!" Joanne recalled, "We hugged, kissed, and cheered André and the Barretts—and the Winiarskis in absentia." She also remembered that both winning winemakers—Mike Grgich and Warren Winiarski— had trained under André.[18]

When *Time* magazine called Grgich from Europe to set up an interview, he knew nothing about the Paris tasting or that his wine was even in the competition. He told the *Time* people to "be sure it's me and not somebody else." On the same day, Grgich received a telegram from Jim Barrett sharing the same news, and Mike could not "understand what [Barrett] was talking about." Within days, however, Grgich started to recognize the tasting's significance. "I finally jumped into the news with that event," Grgich said, "and since then I have been in the news all the time." One year later, Grgich left Chateau Montelena, partnered with Hills Bros. Coffee heir Austin Hills, and established Grgich Hills Cellar in Rutherford. Grgich and Hills broke ground on the Fourth of July 1977. That same year they started building their new winery and began their first crush in September. "We didn't have a roof, but we had tanks and crushing equipment," Mike said. Three years later, at an international wine-tasting competition in Chicago called the Chicago Showdown, Grgich's '77 Chardonnay beat 221 contenders to take first place. The wine journalist Craig Goodwin proclaimed it to be "the best Chardonnay in the world."[19]

Grgich clearly recognized André's impact on his own career. Mike once said, "I was very fortunate to meet with André Tchelistcheff at Beaulieu Vineyard, and even more fortunate that I was accepted to work for him." Warren Winiarski shared Grgich's admiration for Tchelistcheff. In an interview with a *Napa Valley Register* reporter several weeks after the Paris tasting, Winiarski credited both winning wines to the influence of André Tchelistcheff. "I've always admired André's wines," Warren said, so much so that soon after André's contractual obligations to Heublein ended in April 1973, Winiarski hired him to consult for Stag's Leap Wine Cellars. Warren knew of no one who "possessed the two things that I observed about André, the science and the poetry." Warren continued, "I wanted to make poetic wines, but I also wanted to make them commercially correct and superlative." André admired Winiarski as well. He later reflected that Warren represented one of the few winemakers in California who "really understands the wines, who lives with the wines daily, who never separates his wine from himself, and who really gives everything that he has, his mind, his energy, his philosophy, his dreams, to his own products." On a warm September day in 1973, shortly before he officially signed on as Winiarski's consultant, André, accompanied by Dorothy, drove up the Silverado Trail to pay Warren a visit. Winiarski wanted André's input on choosing the right harvest date, so he asked for André's opinion. "We walked through the vineyard," Warren said. "André walked a little ahead of us, and he was picking at the grapes from the clusters and tasting, and he made some remark about honey, divine honey, and I embraced Dorothy." Upon "hearing those words" from a wine master like Tchelistcheff, Winiarski was convinced that "we were at about the right time for harvest." Winiarski's '73 Cabernet Sauvignon, the one that prevailed in the '76 Paris tasting, was sourced from the grapes that tasted like "divine honey."[20]

Winiarski did not participate in the '76 Tchelistcheff tour; instead, he had spent the last week of May in Chicago settling his mother's estate. Dorothy called the Winiarski residence in Napa to share the good news and relayed it to Warren's wife, Barbara. She, in turn, phoned her husband, who responded, "That's nice." Upon some reflection, however, Winiarski soon realized the significance of the Paris tasting. "Nothing was the same after that," Warren said. "It certainly changed the way I looked at things." Warren "felt more responsibility to do the best and to not be unlimited by any artificial barriers to achieving beauty in the wines I was making." In fact, Winiarski began referring to the Paris tasting as a "Copernican moment." Warren was referencing the sixteenth-century Polish mathematician and astronomer

Nicolaus Copernicus, whose posthumously published book, *On the Revolutions of the Heavenly Spheres*, in 1543 postulated a heliocentric, or sun-centered, universe. Copernicus challenged Ptolemaic theory, formulated in the second century of the Common Era by Claudius Ptolemy of Alexandria, that advanced a geocentric, or earth-centered, model. Copernicus imagined a different celestial harmony, reasoning that the Ptolemaic system lacked mathematical rigor and failed to square with his own cosmological observations. The Roman Catholic Church of the era branded the Copernican theory as pure heresy, executed one of its principal adherents, and sentenced another to house arrest. Nonetheless, the subsequent scientific discoveries of Johannes Kepler, Galileo Galilei, and Isaac Newton validated Copernicus's revolutionary hypothesis.[21]

Copernicus combined imagination and mathematical precision to launch a paradigm shift in the world of science. Tchelistcheff applied a similar approach to his own profession. André once said, "Imagination can become lost in the scientific process, but not when there are deep feelings of love. There is no love if there is no imagination ... and no imagination without love." He spent his career bridging imagination with technical exactitude, becoming a consummate winegrower and mentoring others such as Warren Winiarski and Mike Grgich on how to produce wines of subtlety, harmony, and complexity. He also taught all of his many students the value of respect, humility, patience, and responsibility, or—as some of them characterized it—about life in general. As a result, the man later described as "the father of California winemaking" played a pivotal role, if not *the* pivotal role, in Napa Valley's "Copernican moment." The valley's wine industry, along with its counterparts in Washington, Oregon, California's Sonoma County and Central Coast, and northern Tuscany, never looked back.[22]

Notes

PREFACE

1. Heidi Peterson Barrett interview by Charles Sullivan, Napa CA, January 11, 1999, Wine Library Archives (WLA), box 57; Pierce Carson, "Retirement Doesn't Mean He's Been Put Out to Pasture," *Napa Valley Register*, December 15, 1991; Dorothy Tchelistcheff interview by Charles Sullivan, Napa CA, March 30, 1998, St. Helena Public Library, WLA, box 57; and Heublein Fine Wine Group, "Andre Tchelistcheff's Birthday," edited master VHS, December 7, 1991, courtesy of Dorothy Tchelistcheff.
2. Hutchison, "André Tchelistcheff," 27.

1. THE TCHELISTCHEFF TOUR, PART I

1. MacNeil, *Wine Bible*, 696; and Laube, "Rethinking Napa Valley," 36–70.
2. Cited in Esther Mobley, "Hidden Figures behind the Judgment of Paris," *San Francisco Chronicle*, October 28, 2018.
3. Louis M. Martini and Louis P. Martini, "Wine Making in the Napa Valley," oral history conducted by Lois Stone and Ruth Teiser, Regional Oral History Office, Bancroft Library, University of California, Berkeley, 1973.
4. Joanne Dickenson DePuy interview by author, Napa CA, April 15, 2019.
5. Dickenson DePuy interview by author.
6. Dickenson DePuy interview by author. The 1976 Tchelistcheff tour group consisted of Louis P. and Liz Martini; Andy and Betty Beckstoffer; Bob and Nonie Travers; Arthur and Sheila Hailey; Jim and Laura Barrett; René di Rosa and his fiancée, Veronica; Norb and Ruth Mirassou; Ernie and Virginia Van Asperen; Margrit Biever (soon to be Mondavi); George and Gertrude Marsh; Morgen and Pauline Ruddick; Zelma Long; Chris Brix; Wally and Nancy Opdyke; MaryAnn Graf; Katie Spann; Stan and Carol Anderson; Bill and Ann Sorenson; Paul Tchelistcheff (André's grandson); Bern Laxer (official photographer); André and Dorothy Tchelistcheff; and Joanne Dickenson (DePuy).

7. Mobley, "Hidden Figures."
8. Taber, *Judgment of Paris*, 158–61.
9. Dickenson DePuy interview by author.
10. Dickenson DePuy interview by author.
11. Dickenson DePuy interview by author; Mobley, "Hidden Figures"; and Taber, *Judgment of Paris*, 158.
12. Dickenson DePuy interview by author; and Taber, *Judgment of Paris*, 156–62.
13. The American Society of Enologists was formed in 1950. In recognition of its expanded scope, the organization was renamed in 1984. See Pinney, *History of Wine*, 2:429.
14. Bonné, *New California Wine*, 24.
15. Warren Winiarski interview by Charles Sullivan, Napa CA, February 16, 1999, St. Helena Public Library, WLA, box 57.
16. Peterson, *Winemaker*, 152.
17. D. Tchelistcheff interview by Sullivan (see preface, n. 1).
18. Tanzer, "Vertical Tasting," 2.
19. Jill Davis interview by author, Glen Ellen CA, January 13, 2020; Rob Davis interview by author, Healdsburg CA, April 16, 2019; Mike (Miljenko) Grgich interview by Charles Sullivan, Rutherford CA, January 10, 1999, St. Helena Public Library, WLA; and Winiarski interview by Sullivan.
20. Richard (Dick) Peterson interview by Charles Sullivan, Yountville CA, March 31, 1998, St. Helena Public Library, WLA, box 57; Chris Markell interview by author, Windsor CA, March 9, 2020; and Rick Sayre interview by author, Windsor CA, March 9, 2020.
21. André Tchelistcheff, "Grapes, Wine, and Ecology," an interview conducted by Ruth Teiser and Catherine Harroun, 1979, Regional Oral History Office, Bancroft Library, University of California, Berkeley, 19, 94.

2. KALUGA

1. During the Tsarist period, Russia followed the Julian calendar, thirteen days behind the Gregorian one used in the West. In January 1918, the Bolsheviks switched to the Gregorian calendar following their revolutionary takeover of the Russian government.
2. On April 5, 1242, Russian forces led by Prince Alexander Nevsky repulsed an invasion of Teutonic Knights at Lake Peipus. In 1938 filmmaker Sergei Eisenstein commemorated the battle in his patriotic drama *Alexander Nevsky*, a not so subtle effort to link the invasion of Teutonic Knights to the threat posed by Nazi Germany.
3. Tchelistcheff, "Grapes, Wine, and Ecology," 2–3 (see chap. 1, n. 21); and Maria Tchelistcheff, telephone conversation with author, March 11, 2020.

4. Viktor Tchelistcheff, "Going to Mass," unpublished ms., n.d., Tchelistcheff (Dorothy and André) Collection.

5. Dorothy Tchelistcheff interview by author, Napa CA, April 15, 2019; Smith, *Private Reserve*, 98; and Victor Tchelistcheff, Notes, n.d., Tchelistcheff (Dorothy and André) Collection.

6. Dorothy Tchelistcheff interview by author, Napa CA, June 23, 2019.

7. Schmemann, *Echoes of a Native Land*, 4–24.

8. Smith, *Private Reserve*, 98.

9. Cited in McMeekin, *Russian Revolution*, 9.

10. McMeekin, *Russian Revolution*, 16–17.

11. Riasanovsky, *History of Russia*, 450.

12. Riasanovsky and Steinberg, *History of Russia*, 381.

13. Marples, *Lenin's Revolution*, 9.

14. Riasanovsky, *History of Russia*, 451; and Tchelistcheff, "Grapes, Wine, and Ecology," 5.

15. D. Tchelistcheff interview by Sullivan (see preface, n. 1); Tchelistcheff, "Grapes, Wine, and Ecology," 10; and Lord, "André Tchelistcheff," 31.

16. Riasanovsky and Steinberg, *History of Russia*, 359-68.

17. McMeekin, *Russian Revolution*, 41; and Riasanovsky and Steinberg, *History of Russia*, 368–72.

18. Tchelistcheff, "Grapes, Wine, and Ecology," 10; and Tchelistcheff, Notes.

19. McMeekin, *Russian Revolution*, 51.

20. McMeekin, *July 1914*, 273.

21. Quoted in Riasanovsky and Steinberg, *History of Russia*, 424.

22. McMeekin, *Russian Revolution*, 131; and Riasanovsky and Steinberg, *History of Russia*, 424-42. Parentheses in original.

23. Riasanovsky and Steinberg, *History of Russia*, 443; Sixsmith, "Fanny Kaplan's Attempt," in Brenton, *Was Revolution Inevitable?*, 193; and Tchelistcheff, "Grapes, Wine, and Ecology," 6.

24. Tchelistcheff, "Grapes, Wine, and Ecology," 6.

25. Sixsmith, "Fanny Kaplan's Attempt," in Brenton, *Was Revolution Inevitable?*, 196.

26. Darrell Corti, email communications with author, April 22, 2019, and March 1, 2020; and Tchelistcheff, "Grapes, Wine, and Ecology," 6.

27. McMeekin, *Russian Revolution*, 246. On April 13, 1918, a shelling near Ekaterinodar killed Kornilov. Gen. Anton Denikin, another low-born career soldier like Kornilov, replaced him.

28. Tchelistcheff, "Grapes, Wine, and Ecology," 8.

29. Tchelistcheff, "Grapes, Wine, and Ecology," 8–9.

30. McMeekin, *Russian Revolution*, 297.

31. In February 1918, the Bolsheviks, fearful of a foreign invasion, had moved the Russian capital from Petrograd to Moscow.

32. McMeekin, *Russian Revolution*, 294–95.
33. McMeekin, *Russian Revolution*, 290–93; and Mawdsley, *Russian Civil War*, 213.
34. Mawdsley, *Russian Civil War*, 205, 219.
35. Mawdsley, *Russian Civil War*, chap. 19.
36. D. Tchelistcheff interview by author, April 15, 2019.
37. Riasanovsky and Steinberg, *History of Russia*, 453–55; and Mawdsley, *Russian Civil War*, 271.

3. THE APACHE DANCER

1. Tchelistcheff, "Grapes, Wine, and Ecology," 13–14 (see chap. 1, n. 21); and Bronfman, *Legends of Napa Valley*.
2. Gilbert and Large, *End of the European Era*, 152; and Tchelistcheff, "Grapes, Wine, and Ecology," 14.
3. Tchelistcheff, "Grapes, Wine, and Ecology," 14.
4. Tchelistcheff, "Grapes, Wine, and Ecology," 15–16.
5. Gilbert and Large, *End of the European Era*, 157–58.
6. Tchelistcheff, "Grapes, Wine, and Ecology," 16–17, 95.
7. Maria Tchelistcheff conversation with author (see chap. 2, n. 3); and letter from Daniel Orville Dechert to George Tate, vice-consul, American Embassy, Paris, France, January 26, 1938, Tchelistcheff (Dorothy and André) Collection.
8. Tchelistcheff, "Grapes, Wine, and Ecology," 18–23.
9. Tchelistcheff, "Grapes, Wine, and Ecology," 18–20.
10. Lukacs, *Inventing Wine*, 74.
11. MacNeil, *Wine Bible*, 17.
12. Lukacs, *Inventing Wine*, 98–101.
13. Lukacs, *Inventing Wine*, 142–43.
14. De Cassagnac, *French Wines*, 11.
15. Nathan Chroman, "Salute to the Grand Old Man of California Wine Making," *Los Angeles Times*, December 27, 1976, 8.
16. Tchelistcheff, "Grapes, Wine, and Ecology," 23–29.
17. D. Tchelistcheff interview by the author, Napa CA, April 15, 2019; and Michael Hoffman, telephone conversation with author, February 22, 2020.
18. Tchelistcheff, "Grapes, Wine, and Ecology," 24; Nathan Chroman, "Private Tasting Confirms a King," *Los Angeles Times*, June 28, 1981, 43–44; and Chris Markell, email communication with author, September 29, 2020.
19. Tchelistcheff, "Grapes, Wine, and Ecology," 24.
20. André Tchelistcheff with Warren Winiarski interview by Charles L. Sullivan, 1987, audiocassette, Charles L. Sullivan Papers on California Wine History D-346, box 15, Special Collections, Library, University of California, Davis.
21. Tchelistcheff, "Grapes, Wine, and Ecology," 22–24; and A. Tchelistcheff interview by Sullivan.

22. Tchelistcheff, "Grapes, Wine, and Ecology," 24–25.
23. Tchelistcheff, "Grapes, Wine, and Ecology," 25–27; and A. Tchelistcheff interview by Sullivan.
24. Tchelistcheff, "Grapes, Wine, and Ecology," 25–26; Smith, *Private Reserve*, 103–4; Paul Marsais, reference letter, July 20, 1938, Tchelistcheff (Dorothy and André) Collection; and L. M. Fabbrini, "Application for the Admission into the United States of Andre Tchelistcheff," August 17, 1938, Tchelistcheff (Dorothy and André) Collection.
25. Tchelistcheff, "Grapes, Wine, and Ecology," 30–33.
26. Tchelistcheff, "Grapes, Wine, and Ecology," 33–34.
27. Tchelistcheff, "Grapes, Wine, and Ecology," 28–35.

4. BEAUTIFUL PLACE

1. Camp, *George C. Yount*, 221; and Madley, *American Genocide*, 121–22.
2. Teiser and Harroun, *Winemaking in California*, 28–39; and Pinney, *A History of Wine*, 1:269–84.
3. Teiser and Harroun, *Winemaking in California*, 82–83; and Sullivan, *Napa Wine*, 34–35.
4. Sullivan, *Napa Wine*, 59–60; and MacNeill, *Wine Bible*, 675.
5. Sullivan, *Napa Wine*, 60.
6. Sullivan, *Napa Wine*, 77–80; and Teiser and Harroun, *Winemaking in California*, 85.
7. Teiser and Harroun, *Winemaking in California*, 95–97; and Sullivan, *Napa Wine*, 116–18.
8. Sullivan, *Napa Wine*, 162; Smith, *Private Reserve*, 13–20; and A. Tchelistcheff interview by Sullivan (see chap. 4, n. 20).
9. Sullivan, *Napa Wine*, 163; and Smith, *Private Reserve*, 23–51.
10. Smith, *Private Reserve*, 59–75.
11. Lapsley, *Bottled Poetry*, 10–11.
12. Smith, *Private Reserve*, 74.
13. Smith, *Private Reserve*, 83.
14. André Tchelistcheff interview by Richard G. Peterson, Rutherford CA, January 15, 1975, in Napa Valley Wine Library Association, *History of Napa Valley*.
15. Tchelistcheff, "Grapes, Wine, and Ecology," 35–36 (see chap. 1, n. 21).
16. Tchelistcheff, "Grapes, Wine, and Ecology," 35–41.
17. Tchelistcheff, "Grapes, Wine, and Ecology," 41–42; and Conaway, *Napa*, 109.
18. Tchelistcheff, "Grapes, Wine, and Ecology," 42–84; and Tchelistcheff interview by Peterson.
19. Tchelistcheff, "Grapes, Wine, and Ecology," 49–58.

20. Tchelistcheff, "Grapes, Wine, and Ecology," 66; Smith, *Private Reserve*, 177–81; Hutchison, "André Tchelistcheff," 27; and Bob Thompson, "André Tchelistcheff back at Beaulieu," *San Francisco Examiner*, February 6, 1991, 62.

21. Tchelistcheff, "Grapes, Wine, and Ecology," 63–87; Conaway, *Napa*, 108–9; and Hutchison, "André Tchelistcheff," 26.

22. Tchelistcheff, "Grapes, Wine, and Ecology," 63; and Dan Berger, "Andre Tchelistcheff, Master Winemaker, Dies," *Los Angeles Times*, 7 April 1994.

23. Smith, *Private Reserve*, 109–12; and Tchelistcheff, "Grapes, Wine, and Ecology," 89–90.

24. Tchelistcheff, "Grapes, Wine, and Ecology," 79; and Dagmar Sullivan interview by Charles Sullivan, Rutherford CA, January 11, 1999, St. Helena Public Library, WLA, box 57; Walter Sullivan III interview by Charles Sullivan, San Francisco, March 22, 1999, St. Helena Public Library, WLA; and A. Tchelistcheff interview by Sullivan.

25. Smith, *Private Reserve*, 117; Conaway, *Napa*, 109–10; and Tchelistcheff, "Grapes, Wine, and Ecology," 90.

26. Tchelistcheff, "Grapes, Wine, and Ecology," 68–69; and Lapsley, *Bottled Poetry*, 16–17. The "big four" soon became the "big five" with the revival of the Charles Krug Winery under the Mondavi family. See Sullivan, *Napa Wine*, 237.

27. Tchelistcheff, "Grapes, Wine, and Ecology," 94, 105–7; and Chroman, "Private Tasting," 44.

28. Smith, *Private Reserve*, 120–21; and Conaway, *Napa*, 113.

29. Tchelistcheff, "Grapes, Wine, and Ecology," 90–91; and Smith, *Private Reserve*, 114–16.

5. THE MENTOR

1. André Tchelistcheff interview by Margrit Biever Mondavi, Oakville CA, California, March 27, 1990, Tchelistcheff (Dorothy and André) Collection; and Siler, *House of Mondavi*, 9–17.

2. Siler, *House of Mondavi*, 17–24.

3. Robert Mondavi interview by Charles Sullivan, Oakville CA, April 13, 1999, St. Helena Public Library, WLA, box 57.

4. Tchelistcheff, "Grapes, Wine, and Ecology," 90–92 (see chap. 1, n. 21); and Louis P. Martini interview by Charles Sullivan, St. Helena CA, March 31, 1998, St. Helena Public Library, WLA, box 57.

5. Peter Mondavi Sr. interview by Charles Sullivan, St. Helena CA, April 13 and 14, 1999, St. Helena Public Library, WLA, box 57; and Sullivan, *Napa Wine*, 250–52.

6. Tchelistcheff interview by Biever Mondavi; and Mondavi interview by Sullivan.

7. "Death Notice: Helene de Latour," *San Francisco Examiner*, November 22, 1982, 23; Conaway, *Napa*, 115; and Peterson, *Winemaker*, 149.

8. Sullivan interview by Sullivan (see chapter 4, n. 24); Conaway, *Napa*, 113; Peterson interview by Sullivan (see chapter 1, n. 19); and Peterson, *Winemaker*, 149.

9. Joseph E. Heitz, "Creating a Winery in the Napa Valley," an interview conducted in 1985 by Ruth Teiser, Regional Oral History Office, Bancroft Library, University of California, Berkeley, 1–21.

10. Joseph Heitz interview by Charles Sullivan, St. Helena CA, March 30, 1998, St. Helena Public Library, WLA, box 57.

11. Heitz, "Creating a Winery," 21–53.

12. Theo Rosenbrand interview by Charles Sullivan, St. Helena CA, July 22, 1998, St. Helena Public Library, WLA, box 57.

13. D. Tchelistcheff interview by author, April 5, 2019; Rosenbrand interview by Sullivan; and Smith, *Private Reserve*, 124–25. See also chapter 6.

14. Smith, *Private Reserve*, 126–27; Sullivan, *Napa Wine*, 254–55; and Pinney, *History of Wine*, 2:227.

15. Legh F. Knowles, "Beaulieu Vineyard from Family to Corporate Ownership," an interview conducted in 1989 by Lisa Jacobson for the Wine Spectator California Winemen Series, Regional Oral History Office, Bancroft Library, University of California, Berkeley; and Adams, *Wines of America*, 276.

16. Miljenko Grgich, "Miljenko Grgich: A Croatian-American Winemaker in the Napa Valley," an interview conducted in 1992 by Ruth Teiser, Regional Oral History Office, Bancroft Library, University of California, Berkeley, 1–8.

17. Grgich, "Miljenko Grgich," interview by Teiser, 8–15.

18. Grgich, "Miljenko Grgich," interview by Teiser, 17–19.

19. Mike (Miljenko) Grgich interview by Charles Sullivan, Rutherford CA, September 10, 1998, and January 10, 1999, St. Helena Public Library, WLA, box 57.

20. Siler, *House of Mondavi*, 43–56; and Frank J. Prial, "Robert Mondavi, Napa Wine Champion, Dies at 94," *New York Times*, May 17, 2008.

21. Grgich, "Miljenko Grgich," interview by Teiser, 19–24.

22. Winiarski interview by Sullivan (see chap. 1, n. 14).

23. Warren Winiarski, "Creating Classic Wines in the Napa Valley," an interview conducted in 1991 and 1993 by Ruth Teiser, Regional Oral History Office, Bancroft Library, University of California, Berkeley, 2–10.

24. Winiarski, "Creating Classic Wines," 10–20.

25. Winiarski, "Creating Classic Wines," 20–34; and Sullivan, *Napa Wine*, 242–43.

26. Winiarski, "Creating Classic Wines," 34–36.

6. HEUBLEIN

1. Tchelistcheff, "Grapes, Wine, and Ecology," 120–30 (see chap. 1, n. 21); and Pinney, *History of Wine*, 2:346.

2. Tchelistcheff, "Grapes, Wine, and Ecology," 68; and Robin Lail, email communication with author, May 23, 2020.
3. Conaway, *Napa*, 39–80; and Sullivan, *Napa Wine*, 276.
4. Conaway, *Napa*, 129–30; and Sullivan, *Napa Wine*, 277.
5. Conaway, *Napa*, 93–100; Sullivan, *Napa Wine*, 277; and "John Daniel, Valley Wine Figure, Dies," *Napa Valley Register*, July 14, 1970.
6. Smith, *Private Reserve*, 132; Sullivan interview by Sullivan (see chap. 4, note 24); and Susan Merle and Barbara Stone interview by Charles Sullivan, Napa CA, January 10, 1999, St. Helena Public Library, WLA, box 57.
7. Smith, *Private Reserve*, 132; and Merle and Stone interview by Sullivan.
8. Merle and Stone interview by Sullivan; and D. Tchelistcheff interview by Sullivan (see preface, n. 1).
9. Sullivan interview by Sullivan; R. Davis interview by author (see chap. 1, n. 19); D. Tchelistcheff interview by Sullivan; and D. Tchelistcheff interview by author, June 23, 2019.
10. J. Davis interview by author (see chap. 1, n. 19); and D. Tchelistcheff interview by author, April 15, 2019.
11. Peterson, *Winemaker*, 49–142; and Peterson interview by Sullivan (see chapter 1, n. 20).
12. Peterson, *Winemaker*, 143–50.
13. Peterson, *Winemaker*, 151–52.
14. Peterson interview by Sullivan; and Peterson, *Winemaker*, 151–54.
15. Peterson, *Winemaker*, 164–65.
16. Peterson interview by Sullivan, September 9, 1998; and Peterson, *Winemaker*, 154–94.
17. Tchelistcheff, "Grapes, Wine, and Ecology," 119.
18. Conaway, *Napa*, 134–35.
19. Conaway, *Napa*, 135–37; and Tchelistcheff, "Grapes, Wine, and Ecology," 122.
20. Peterson, *Winemaker*, 195; Conaway, *Napa*, 139, 156; and Andrew Beckstoffer interview by Charles Sullivan, Rutherford CA, July 22, 1998, St. Helena Public Library, WLA, box 57.
21. Tchelistcheff, "Grapes, Wine, and Ecology," 123–24.
22. Peterson, *Winemaker*, 199–200.
23. Peterson, *Winemaker*, 200–201.
24. Conaway, *Napa*, 142–44; and Peterson, *Winemaker*, 204, 213–14.
25. Peterson, *Winemaker*, 215–16; and Peterson interview by Sullivan, September 10, 1998.
26. Fish, "Classic Wines, Treasured Vines," 42–49.
27. Peterson, *Winemaker*, 217–18; Peterson interview by Sullivan, September 10, 1998; and Conaway, *Napa*, 159–60.

28. Beckstoffer interview by Sullivan; and Robert (Bob) Steinhauer interview by Charles Sullivan, St. Helena CA, September 9, 1998, St. Helena Public Library, WLA, box 57.

29. Beckstoffer interview by Sullivan; and Andy Beckstoffer, telephone conversations with author, March 10 and 11, 2020.

30. Smith, *Private Reserve*, 142.

31. Conaway, *Napa*, 157; and Smith, *Private Reserve*, 141–43.

32. Conaway, *Napa*, 157–58; Smith, *Private Reserve*, 143–46; Steinhauer interview by Sullivan; and Tchelistcheff, "Grapes, Wine, and Ecology," 156.

7. THE CONSULTANT

1. Tchelistcheff, "Grapes, Wine, and Ecology," 155–60 (see chap. 1, n. 21).

2. Tchelistcheff, "Grapes, Wine, and Ecology," 157; and MaryAnn Graf, "The Life of a Wine Industry Trailblazer," an interview by Martin Meeker, 2017, Regional Oral History Office, Bancroft Library, University of California, Berkeley, 52.

3. Graf, "Wine Industry Trailblazer," 52–57.

4. Tchelistcheff, "Grapes, Wine, and Ecology," 180–82.

5. Alison Green Doran, telephone conversation with author, February 17, 2020.

6. J. Davis interview by author (see chap. 6, n. 10).

7. J. Davis interview by author.

8. R. Davis interview by author (see chap. 1, n. 19).

9. Tchelistcheff, "Grapes, Wine, and Ecology," 181–83.

10. R. Davis interview by author (see chap. 1, n. 19).

11. R. Davis interview by author.

12. R. Davis interview by author.

13. Tchelistcheff interview by Peterson (see chap. 4, n. 14).

14. R. Davis interview by author.

15. R. Davis interview by author.

16. R. Davis interview by author; and Tchelistcheff, Tony Austin, and Mike Hoffman interview by Chris Whitcraft, Jim Frolek, Frank Ostini, and Bob Senn, Santa Barbara CA, October 19, 1980, KTMS-FM, audiotape, courtesy of Dorothy Tchelistcheff.

17. Sayre interview by author (see chap. 1, n. 19); and Markell interview by author (see chap. 1, n. 19).

18. Sayre interview by author; and Markell interview by author.

19. Tchelistcheff, "Grapes, Wine, and Ecology," 172–73.

20. Tchelistcheff, "Grapes, Wine, and Ecology," 173–76; and Michael Hoffman, telephone conversation with author, February 22, 2020.

21. Tchelistcheff, "Grapes, Wine, and Ecology," 157; Adams, *Wines of America*, 410; and Perdue, "20 Years Later," 2.

22. Blecha, *Chateau Ste. Michelle*, 36–40.
23. Blecha, *Chateau Ste. Michelle*, 40–107.
24. Cheryl Barber Jones interview with author, Woodinville WA, February 3, 2020; and Kay Simon interview with author, Woodinville WA, February 3, 2020.
25. Jones interview by author; and Simon interview by author.
26. Doug Gore, telephone conversation with author, February 3, 2020.
27. Alex Golitzin, telephone conversation with author, February 25, 2020.
28. Tchelistcheff, "Grapes, Wine, and Ecology," 199–200; and Steiman, "Oregon Wine Pioneer."
29. Darrell Corti, telephone conversation with author, March 4, 2020; and Steven Spurrier, "Lodovico and Piero Antinori—*Decanter* Interview," *Decanter*, July 14, 2008.
30. Jerry Mead, "Mourning the Loss of a Legend," *Oakland Tribune*, April 13, 1994; Jack Davies and Jamie Peterman Davies, "Rebuilding Schramsberg: The Creation of a California Champagne House," an interview conducted by Ruth Teiser and Lisa Jacobson, 1989, Regional Oral History Office, Bancroft Library, University of California, Berkeley, 190; and Tchelistcheff, "Grapes, Wine, and Ecology," 170.
31. D. Tchelistcheff interview by author, June 23, 2019.
32. Tchelistcheff interview by Peterson (see chap. 4, n. 14); and Mendelson, *Appellation Napa Valley*, 61.
33. Sullivan, *Napa Wine*, 338; Conaway, *Far Side of Eden*; and Pinney, *History of Wine in America*, 2:243–45.
34. Tchelistcheff interview by Biever Mondavi (see chap. 5, n. 1); and Dan Berger, "Assessing the Tchelistcheff Effect," *Los Angeles Times*, April 14, 1994.
35. Robert L. Balzar, "André Tchelistcheff: An Appreciation," *Los Angeles Times*, April 14, 1994.
36. Tim Tesconi, "Memorial for the Maestro," *Napa Valley Register*, April 12, 1994.

8. THE TCHELISTCHEFF TOUR, PART 2

1. Dickenson DePuy, *Rest of the Story*, 10–11; and Lord, "André Tchelistcheff," 32.
2. Lichine, *Alexis Lichine's Guide*, 375.
3. Kladstrup and Kladstrup, *Wine and War*, 86–88; and Coates, *Encyclopedia*, 540.
4. Tchelistcheff, "Grapes, Wine, and Ecology," 158 (see chap. 1, n. 21); MacNeil, *Wine Bible*, 37; and Lichine, *Alexis Lichine's Guide*, 369.
5. Lichine, *Alexis Lichine's Guide*, 121–22, 171–72; MacNeil, *Wine Bible*, 204–5; and Andy Beckstoffer, telephone conversation with author, March 11, 2020.
6. Beckstoffer interview by Sullivan (see chap. 6, n 20); Dickenson DePuy, *Rest of the Story*, 11; and Dickenson DePuy interview with author (see chap. 1, n. 4).

7. Dickenson DePuy, *Rest of the Story*, 11; Beckstoffer interview by Sullivan; and Martini interview by Sullivan (see chap. 5, n. 3).

8. Kladstrup and Kladstrup, *Wine and War*, 29, 45–47.

9. Kladstrup and Kladstrup, *Wine and War*, 141–43; and Vinen, *Unfree French*, 143.

10. Frank J. Prial, "Alexis Lichine, 76, an Author and Expert on Wine," *New York Times*, June 2, 1989.

11. Dickenson DePuy, *Rest of the Story*, 12; and Taber, *Judgment of Paris*, 206–7.

12. Taber, *Judgment of Paris*, 165–96.

13. Taber, *Judgment of Paris*, 155–63.

14. Taber, *Judgment of Paris*, 199–200.

15. Taber, *Judgment of Paris*, 200–201.

16. Taber, *Judgment of Paris*, 202.

17. Taber, *Judgment of Paris*, 203–5.

18. Dickenson DePuy, *Rest of the Story*, 12–13.

19. Grgich, "Miljenko Grgich," interview by Teiser, 25–29 (see chap. 5, n. 15).

20. Steve Hart, "French Judge Napa Wines Best," *Napa Valley Register*, June 11, 1976; Tchelistcheff, "Grapes, Wine, and Ecology," 190; and Gaiter, "Warren Winiarski."

21. Gaiter, "Warren Winiarski."

22. Balzar, "André Tchelistcheff."

Bibliography

ARCHIVAL AND UNPUBLISHED SOURCES

Bancroft Library, University of California, Berkeley. Regional Oral History Office, California Wine Industry Oral History Project.

    Davies, Jack, and Jamie Peterman Davies. "Rebuilding Schramsberg: The Creation of a California Champagne House." Interview by Ruth Teiser and Lisa Jacobson. 1989.

    Graf, MaryAnn. "The Life of a Wine Industry Trailblazer." Interview by Martin Meeker. 2017.

    Grgich, Miljenko. "Miljenko Grgich: A Croatian-American Winemaker in the Napa Valley." Interview by Ruth Teiser. 1992.

    Heitz, Joseph E. "Creating a Winery in the Napa Valley." Interview by Ruth Teiser. 1985.

    Knowles, Legh F. "Beaulieu Vineyards from Family to Corporate Ownership." Interview by Lisa Jacobsen. 1989.

    Martini, Louis M., and Louis P. Martini. "Wine Making in the Napa Valley." Interview by Lois Stone and Ruth Teiser. 1973.

    Mondavi, Peter. "Advances in Technology and Production at Charles Krug Winery, 1946–1988." Interview by Ruth Teiser. 1988.

    Mondavi, Robert. "Creativity in the California Wine Industry." Interview by Ruth Teiser. 1984.

    Tchelistcheff, André. "Grapes, Wine, and Ecology." Interview by Ruth Teiser and Catherine Harroun. 1979.

    Winiarski, Warren. "Creating Classic Wines in the Napa Valley." Interviews by Ruth Teiser. 1991 and 1993.

Bronfman, Adam R. *The Legends of Napa Valley/America's Foremost Wine Personalities*. VHS. Los Angeles: First Run Video, 1989.

Dickenson DePuy, Joanne. *The Rest of the Story: The Paris Tasting*. Napa CA. 2017. Courtesy of Joanne Dickenson DePuy.

Heublein Fine Wine Group. "Andre Tchelistcheff's Birthday." Edited Master VHS. December 7, 1991. Courtesy of Dorothy Tchelistcheff.

St. Helena Public Library. Wine Library Archives, Box 57. St. Helena CA.

Amaral, Bill. Interview by Charles Sullivan. St. Helena CA. April 14, 1999.

Beckstoffer, Andrew. Interview by Charles Sullivan. Rutherford CA. July 22, 1998.

Grgich, Mike (Miljenko). Interviews by Charles Sullivan. Rutherford CA. September 10, 1998, and January 10, 1999.

Heitz, Joseph. Interview by Charles Sullivan. St. Helena CA. March 30, 1998.

Martini, Louis P. Interview by Charles Sullivan. St. Helena CA. March 31, 1998.

Merle, Susan, and Barbara Stone. Interview by Charles Sullivan. Napa CA. January 10, 1999.

Mondavi, Peter, Sr. Interviews by Charles Sullivan. St. Helena CA. April 13 and 14, 1999.

Mondavi, Robert. Interview by Charles Sullivan. Oakville CA. April 13, 1999.

Peterson, Richard (Dick). Interviews by Charles Sullivan. Yountville CA. March 31, September 9, and September 10, 1998.

Peterson Barrett, Heidi, and Holly Peterson Mondavi. Interview by Charles Sullivan. Napa CA. January 11, 1999.

Rosenbrand, Theo. Interview by Charles Sullivan. St. Helena CA. July 22, 1998.

Steinhauer, Robert (Bob). Interview by Charles Sullivan. St. Helena CA. September 9, 1998.

Sullivan, Dagmar. Interview by Charles Sullivan. Rutherford CA. January 11, 1999.

Sullivan III, Walter. Interview by Charles Sullivan. San Francisco CA. March 22, 1999.

Tchelistcheff, Dorothy. Interview by Charles Sullivan. Napa CA. March 30, 1998.

Winiarski, Warren. Interview by Charles Sullivan. Napa CA. February 16, 1999.

Sullivan, Charles L. Papers on California Wine History, D-346, Box 15. Special Collections, Library, University of California, Davis.

Tchelistcheff, André, with Warren Winiarski. Interview by Charles L. Sullivan. 1987. Audiocassette.

Tchelistcheff (Dorothy and André) Collection, D-654, Box 1. Archives and Special Collections, UC-Davis Library, University of California, Davis.

Dechert, Daniel Orville. Correspondence with George Tate, Vice-Consul, American Embassy, Paris, France. January 26, 1938.

BIBLIOGRAPHY

Fabbrini, L. M. "Application for the Admission into the United States of Andre Tchelistcheff." August 17, 1938.

Marsais, Paul. Reference letter for André Tchelistcheff. July 20, 1938. Tchelistcheff (Dorothy and André) Collection.

Tchelistcheff, André. Interview by Margrit Biever Mondavi. Oakville CA. March 27, 1990. Audiotape.

Tchelistcheff, Viktor. "Going to Mass." Unpublished manuscript. n.d.

Tchelistcheff, André, Tony Austin, and Mike Hoffman. Interview by Chris Whitcraft, Jim Frolek, Frank Ostini, and Bob Senn. Santa Barbara CA. October 19, 1980. KTMS-FM audiotape. Courtesy of Dorothy Tchelistcheff.

Tchelistcheff, Victor. Notes. n.d. Courtesy of Dorothy Tchelistcheff.

PUBLISHED SOURCES

Adams, Leon D. *The Wines of America.* 4th ed. New York: McGraw-Hill, 1990.

Blecha, Peter. *Chateau Ste. Michelle: The First 50 Years, 1967–2017.* Seattle: History Link/Documentary Media, 2017.

Bonné, Jon. *The New California Wine: A Guide to the Producers and Wines behind a Revolution in Taste.* Berkeley CA: Ten Speed Press, 2013.

Camp, Charles L., ed. *George C. Yount and His Chronicles of the West.* Denver: Old West Publishing, 1966.

Coates, Clive. *An Encyclopedia of the Wines and Domaines of France.* Berkeley: University of California Press, 2000.

Conaway, James. *The Far Side of Eden: New Money, Old Land, and the Battle for Napa Valley.* Boston: Houghton Mifflin, 2002.

———. *Napa at Last Light: America's Eden in an Age of Calamity.* New York: Simon & Schuster, 2018.

———. *Napa: The Story of an American Eden.* Boston: Houghton Mifflin, 1990.

De Cassagnac, Paul. *French Wines.* London: Chatto & Windus, 1930.

Fish, Tim. "Classic Wines, Treasured Vines." *Wine Spectator,* June 15, 2017.

Gaiter, Dorothy. "Warren Winiarski Looking Back at the Judgment of Paris." *Grape Collective,* March 18, 2016.

Gilbert, Felix, and David Clay Large. *The End of the European Era: 1890 to the Present.* 6th ed. New York: W. W. Norton, 2009.

Hutchison, John N. "André Tchelistcheff: Man of the Year." *Wines & Vines,* March 1990, 24–29.

Kladstrup, Don, and Petie Kladstrup. *Wine and War: The French, the Nazis and the Battle for France's Greatest Treasure.* New York: Broadway Books, 2002.

Lapsley, James T. *Bottled Poetry: Napa Winemaking from Prohibition to the Modern Era.* Berkeley: University of California Press, 1996. http://ark.cdlib.org/ark:/13030/ft6t1nb4cw/.

167

Laube, James. "Rethinking Napa Valley: The Kingdom of Cabernet Is Breaking Apart, but Making Grander Wines." *Wine Spectator*, 2000, 36–70.

Lichine, Alexis. *Alexis Lichine's Guide to the Wines and Vineyards of France*. 4th ed. New York: Alfred A. Knopf, 1989.

Lord, Tony. "André Tchelistcheff, Decanter's Man of the Year, 1992." *Decanter* 17, no. 7 (March 1992): 31–36.

Lukacs, Paul. *Inventing Wine*. New York: W. W. Norton, 2012.

MacNeil, Karen. *The Wine Bible*. 2nd ed. New York: Workman Publishing, 2015.

Madley, Benjamin. *An American Genocide: The United States and the California Indian Catastrophe*. New Haven CT: Yale University Press, 2017.

Marples, David. *Lenin's Revolution: Russia, 1917–1921*. Harlow, England: Pearson Education, 2000.

Mawdsley, Evan. *The Russian Civil War*. Boston: Allen & Unwin, 1987.

McMeekin, Sean. *July 1914: Countdown to War*. New York: Basic Books, 2013.

———. *The Russian Revolution: A New History*. New York: Basic Books, 2017.

Mendelson, Richard. *Appellation Napa Valley: Building and Protecting an American Treasure*. Napa CA: Val de Grâce Books, 2016.

Napa Valley Wine Library Association, ed. *History of Napa Valley: Interviews and Reminiscences of Long-Time Residents*. Rutherford CA: Napa Valley Wine Library Association, 1975.

Perdue, Andy. "20 Years Later, André Tchelistcheff's Influence Remains in Washington." *Great Northwest Wine*, April 21, 2014, 1–2.

Peterson, Richard G. *The Winemaker*. Middletown CA: Meadowlark Publishing, 2015.

Pinney, Thomas. *A History of Wine in America*. Vol. 1, *From Beginnings to Prohibition*. Berkeley: University of California Press, 1989.

———. *A History of Wine in America*. Vol. 2, *From Prohibition to the Present*. Berkeley: University of California Press, 2005.

Pipes, Richard. *The Russian Revolution*. New York: Vintage Books, 1990.

Riasanovsky, Nicholas V. *A History of Russia*. 4th ed. New York: Oxford University Press, 1984.

Riasanovsky, Nicholas V., and Mark D. Steinberg. *A History of Russia*. 9th ed. New York: Oxford University Press, 2019.

Schmemann, Serge. *Echoes of a Native Land: Two Centuries of a Russian Village*. New York: Alfred A. Knopf, 1997.

Siler, Julia Flynn. *The House of Mondavi: The Rise and Fall of an American Wine Dynasty*. New York: Gotham Books, 2007.

Sixsmith, Martin. "Fanny Kaplan's Attempt to Kill Lenin: August 1918." In *Was Revolution Inevitable? Turning Points of the Russian Revolution*, edited by Tony Brenton, 178–200. New York: Oxford University Press, 2017.

Smith, Rod. *Private Reserve: Beaulieu Vineyard and the Rise of Napa Valley*. Stamford CT: Daglan Press, 2000.

Spurrier, Steven. "Lodovico and Piero Antinori—*Decanter* Interview." *Decanter*, July 14, 2008.

Steiman, Harvey. "Oregon Wine Pioneer David Lett Dies." *Wine Spectator*, October 13, 2008.

Sullivan, Charles L. *Napa Wine: A History*. 2nd ed. San Francisco: Napa Valley Wine Library Association, 2008.

Taber, George M. *Judgment of Paris: California vs. France and the Historic Paris Tasting That Revolutionized Wine*. New York: Scribner, 2005.

Tanzer, Stephen. "Vertical Tasting of Beaulieu Vineyard's Georges de Latour Private Reserve Cabernet Sauvignon: 1965–2016." *Vinous*, April 11, 2019.

Teiser, Ruth, and Catherine Harroun. *Winemaking in California*. New York: McGraw-Hill, 1983.

Vinen, Richard. *The Unfree French: Life under the Occupation*. London: Penguin Books, 2007.

Index

quality of wines from, 42–44, 60,
61, 86, 149; Tchelistcheffs' trips to,
96, 98; transporting wine to, 7, 8;
and White Army, 28, 31, 33, 35; wine
consultants in, 124; wine industry
in, xi, 41–42, 116; winemaking
methods in, 63, 100; wine tasting in,
6, 8, 146–49; wine tours in, xiii, 4–7,
125, 137, 139, 142
Franciscan Estate, 133
Freemark Abbey, 6, 8, 99, 146, 148
French language, 37, 40, 49, 142
French Limousin barrels, 78
French Resistance, 141
French Revolution, 42, 142
Fresno CA, 77
Fresno State University, 78, 109
frost protection, 84
Fundamental Laws, 22

Galileo Galilei, 152
Gallipoli, 35–36
Gamay Beaujolais, 106, 121
Gapon, Georgy, 21
Gastaud-Gallagher, Patricia, 5, 6, 146,
147, 148
Gaul, 41
Gaulle, Charles de, 68
Gault & Millau, 147
Genoa, Italy, 2
Georges de Latour Private Reserve
Cabernet Sauvignon: fining of, 77–
78; popularity of, 66, 81; production
under Heublein, 106–7, 111; vinegar
from, 100–101
Georges de Latour Private Reserve
Cabernet Sauvignon (1947): gift of,
xi; quality of, 69; spared in fire, 69
Georgia-Pacific, 104
German language, 37, 53

Germany: André Tchelistcheff's
forebear from, 13; attitude toward
Vladimir Lenin, 25; control of
French wineries, 140, 144; in
Czechoslovakia, 38; immigrants
from, 53, 54; Mike Grgich in, 83;
outpost on Ukrainian border, 29;
Russian treaty with, 28; Russian
war with, 23; wine industry in, xi,
41; withdrawal from Russian, 31. *See
also* Nazism
Gewurztraminer, 127
Gironde estuary, 145
Glenn Miller Orchestra, 82
Gogh, Vincent van, 139
Golden Gate International Exposition
(1939), 66
Golitzin, Alex, 131
Golitzin, Alexandra Tchelistcheff, 26,
38, 131
Golitzin, Jeannette, 131
Golitzin, Paul, 131
Golitzin, Peter, 131
Gomel, Ukraine, 29
Goodwin, Craig, 150
Gore, Doug, 130–31
Gorna-Dzhumaya, Bulgaria, 36
Graf, MaryAnn, 114–15
Grand Cru Burgundy, 121, 141
grape growing: André Tchelistcheff's
approach to, 68, 100, 111, 151, 152;
California regions for, 134–35; by
Cistercians, 41; climate for, 1, 2, 65,
91; at Clos de Vougeot, 142; cost of,
106–7; early efforts in Napa Valley,
51, 52; estates for, 42; European
methods of, 10, 54, 61–62, 65;
problems of, 43, 56–57, 108; relation
to winemaking, 10, 65, 100, 109, 110,
111, 115–17. *See also* viticulture and
enology

grapes: planting in Napa Valley, 54;
   planting in Oregon, 132; production
   in Washington State, 127, 128,
   131; sales of, 71, 94–95; used in
   BV wines, 105–7. *See also specific
   varietals*
Grapes into Wine (Wagner), 88
Graves, 143
Great Britain, 7, 28, 30–33, 75, 81, 141, 145
Greek troops, 31
Green, Russell (Russ), 114–16
Grenache, 54, 127, 135
Grenache rosé, 127
Grgich, Miljenko (Mike): André
   Tchelistcheff's influence on, 11,
   84–85, 150, 152; award-winning
   wines of, 150; at BV, 82–84; at
   Chateau Montelena, 86, 146; at
   Mondavi winery, 85, 86
Grgich Hills Cellar, 150
Grignolino grapevines, 78
Guide to California Wines (Melville), 81

Hahn, Ernie, 86
Haigh, Isabelle Simi, 113–14
Hanzell Vineyards, 78
Haraszthy, Agoston, 52–53
Harkin, Earl, 7, 8
Harris, Henry, 58
Hartford CT, 94, 103
Harvey's Bristol Cream sherry, 94
Haut-Médoc, 143, 144, 145
Hawthorne CA, 76
Healdsburg CA, 57, 58, 113–15
Heitz, Alice, 77, 78, 79
Heitz, Joseph, xii, 76–79, 134, 146
Heitz Wine Cellars, 6, 78
Hennessy Cognac, 141
Heublein Fine Wine Group: André
   Tchelistcheff's contract with,
   150; business plan for BV, 105–7,

110, 111; consulting for, 108, 110,
   133; president of, xi; purchase of
   Inglenook, 94–95, 102; takeover of
   BV, xiii, 103–5
Hiaring, Phil, 137
Hills, Austin, 150
Hills Bros. Coffee, 150
Hiroaka, Roy, 75
Hoffman, David, 125–26
Hoffman, Jennifer Andra, 126
Hoffman, Michael, 125, 126
Hoffman, Stanley, 125–26
Hoffman, Terry, 126
Hoffman Mountain Ranch, 45, 125, 126
Holt property, 78
Horse Heaven Hills, 131
horses, 15, 26
Hotel George V, 68
Howell Mountain, 89
Howell Mountain AVA, 134
Hungary, 39, 40, 52

Ile-de-France, 48
Illinois, 76, 87
I. Magnin and Company, 85
Imperial Jurists Association, 13
Inglenook: consulting for, 74;
   ownership and management of, 59,
   92, 93, 95, 102, 107, 108; phylloxera
   at, 55; reputation of, 67, 68, 92–95;
   Spurriers' decline to tour, 6; success
   of, 55–56, 81; winemakers from,
   70, 73
Institute of Agricultural Technology,
   37, 39
Institute of Appellations of Origin, xi
Institute of National Agronomy, xiii,
   40, 43–46
Intercontinental Hotel, 146
An Invitation to Wine (Storm), 88
Iowa, 98

U.S. Army Air Corps, 72
U.S. Army Air Forces, 3, 82
U.S. Army National Guard, 99
U.S. Tobacco of Connecticut, 128

Vaca Mountains, 1
Vallejo, Mariano Guadalupe, 52
Vallerga's Market, 4
Valley of the Queen Hospital, 137
Vancouver College, 83
Vannequé, Christian, 147, 149
Veedercrest Vineyard, 146
Vélodrome d'Hiver, 144
Viala, Pierre, 43–45, 56
Villa, "Pancho," 48, 49
Villages region (France), 121
Villaine, Aubert de, 6, 147
Villa Mt. Eden Winery, 133
vinegar, 100–101, 141
Vinexpo, 132
Vinifera Development Corporation,
    107, 108, 109
vinifera grapes and wines, 54, 127, 128,
    132
Vin Rouge Ordinaire, 121
Vintners Hall of Fame, 9
viticulture and enology: André
    Tchelistcheff's love of, 115, 140;
    André Tchelistcheff's training
    in, 40, 43–44, 65; comparison of
    European and American, 49–50;
    importance to California economy,
    56; scientific contributions to, 141.
    See also grape growing; winemaking
Vitis rupestris. See St. George rootstock
vodka, 94, 95, 98, 107
Volstead Act (1919), 9. *See also*
    Prohibition
Voltaire, 147
Vrinat, Jean-Claude, 147

Wagner, Philip, 88
Waldorf Astoria, 68
Wappo, 51–52
Washington DC, 82
Washington State, xiii, 98, 115, 127–32, 152
Washington State University, 128, 129
Washington Wine Hall of Fame, 130
Watson, Stuart, 94, 102–4, 111
Watson, William C., 55
Wente, Ernest, 60
Wente brothers, 58, 59, 61
Wente "Sauternes, Valle d'Oro," 46
White Army, 10, 27–36
White House, 68, 81, 85, 134
White Riesling, 54, 127
White Russians, 16, 29
white wines: fermentation of, 10,
    67, 101; Mondavis' production of
    BV, 73; at Paris wine tasting, 146,
    148–49; popularity of Bordeaux, 42,
    43; quality of California, 61, 74, 86,
    146; in Washington State, 127, 129
Wild Horse Valley AVA, 134
Willamette Valley, 132
wine: André Tchelistcheff's impression
    of BV's, 48; bulk sales of, 58, 59, 67,
    72, 92, 93, 94; chemical composition
    of, 42; grapes used for BV, 105;
    poetry of, 120–21, 130, 137, 151;
    sacramental uses of, 48, 58–60;
    sales of Inglenook generic, 95;
    sales trends of, 81, 135; "snob" factor
    of, 99; tasting of young, 130; in
    Tchelistcheff family, 40; vineyard
    designated, 79. *See also* champagne;
    red wines; rosé wines; viticulture
    and enology; white wines; *and
    specific varietals*
Wine Advisory Board, 82
Wine Advocate, 131

IN THE AT TABLE SERIES

The Food and Cooking
of Eastern Europe
Lesley Chamberlain
With a new introduction
by the author

The Food and Cooking of Russia
Lesley Chamberlain
With a new introduction
by the author

The World on a Plate: A Tour through
the History of America's Ethnic Cuisine
Joel Denker

Jewish American Food Culture
Jonathan Deutsch and Rachel D. Saks

The Recipe Reader: Narratives,
Contexts, Traditions
Edited by Janet Floyd
and Laurel Forster

A Chef's Tale: A Memoir of
Food, France, and America
Pierre Franey
With Richard Flaste and Bryan Miller
With a new introduction
by Eugenia Bone

Masters of American Cookery:
M. F. K. Fisher, James Beard,
Craig Claiborne, Julia Child
Betty Fussell
With a preface by the author

My Kitchen Wars: A Memoir
Betty Fussell
With a new introduction
by Laura Shapiro

Good Things
Jane Grigson

Jane Grigson's Fruit Book
Jane Grigson
With a new introduction
by Sara Dickerman

Jane Grigson's Vegetable Book
Jane Grigson
With a new introduction
by Amy Sherman

Dining with Marcel Proust:
A Practical Guide to French
Cuisine of the Belle Epoque
Shirley King
Foreword by James Beard

Pampille's Table: Recipes and
Writings from the French
Countryside from Marthe Daudet's
Les Bons Plats de France
Translated and adapted
by Shirley King

Moveable Feasts: The History,
Science, and Lore of Food
Gregory McNamee